STORIES *from* TORY ISLAND

Dorothy Harrison Therman

First published in hardback in 1989
by
Country House

This edition
(unaltered but with a revised introduction)
published in 1999 by
Town House Publishers
Trinity House, Charleston Rd
Ranelagh, Dublin 6

ISBN: 1-86059-084-5

Copyright © Dorothy Harrison Therman 1989

Introduction © Dorothy Harrison Therman 1999

All rights reserved. No part of this publication may be copied, reproduced, stored in a retrieval system, broadcast or transmitted in any form or by any means, electronic, mechanical, photocopying, recording or otherwise without prior permission in writing from the publishers.

A CIP catalogue record for this book is available from the British Library.

Typeset by Typeform Repro, Dublin

Printed in the UK by Caledonian Book Manufacturing, Glasgow

Cover illustration: *The Tau cross on Tory Island* (1989), Derek Hill

Contents

ACKNOWLEDGEMENTS *v*

FOREWORD *Derek Hill* *vii*

PREFACE *xi*

INTRODUCTION *xxi*

DÓNAL DOOHAN *1*

MARY MCCLAFFERTY *52*

DAN RODGERS *79*

MADGE RODGERS *104*

PÁDRAIG ÓG RODGERS *108*

GRÁINNE BHRIANAÍ DOOHAN *134*

PATSY DAN RODGERS *165*

EPILOGUE *178*

BIBLIOGRAPHY *179*

INDEX *181*

Acknowledgements

My thanks to Sean Popplewell, who introduced me to the Tory Island paintings and is, therefore, wholly responsible for this book. To Dónal Doohan, Pádraig Óg Rodgers, Dan Rodgers, Mary McClafferty, Madge Rodgers, Gráinne Bhrianaí Doohan and Patsy Dan Rodgers, the storytellers, and to those on Tory, including William Rodgers, who contributed additional information. To Eilish Rodgers, who, during all my visits to the island, has provided me with generous board and lodging and a hot-water bottle in my bed every night. To Sean Ó hEochaidh and Hugh Curran for their delightful supplementary material. To Séamas Ó Cathain for letting me browse in the library and archives of the Folklore Department at University College, Dublin, and who has kindly corrected my spelling of certain Irish words. To Enda Cunningham of Cathach Books, an always hospitable source of antiquarian information and cups of coffee. To Professor Henry Glassie for his advice to 'listen to the silences'. To Derek Hill for his moral support and encouragement. To Edward Claflin for some very helpful editorial suggestions. To my son and daughter-in-law and a variety of good friends in America and Ireland, who were convinced that I could be an author long before I imagined such a possibility. To Frank Convery who, more than once, has played the role of 'fairy godfather'. To Debbie Smith, who typed many revisions of the manuscript and never complained, in spite of untidy additions and corrections and strange Irish words; and to Treasa Coady who, because of her love of Irish heritage, decided to publish these stories of a time long past on Tory Island.

Foreword

Judging by the time difference, it must have been in the afternoon that I was sitting at my desk at St Columb's in County Donegal, where I then lived, looking out of the Morris-wallpaper-framed window onto Lake Gartan, when the telephone rang. 'This is Dorothy Therman from Philadelphia speaking. It's early morning here and you won't know me. I wish to help Tory Island and would like to give them five thousand pounds — what shall I do with it?' 'Send a cheque to the bank,' was my immediate reply, and from that moment on I realised what a staunch and loyal friend the island had got.

Every year Dorothy goes there, sometimes even twice, and there is not a house she has not visited and not a living soul who is not grateful to Dorothy for her help. Her support consists of sound advice and financial assistance when she feels some enterprise needs her. Dorothy is tall and elegant, well brought up and accustomed to a luxurious lifestyle; that never interferes, however, with what she plans and wants to do — usually for other people. Her clenching and unclenching of her hands when she talks demonstrates a great determination and iron will. I can think of nobody else who could have helped the islanders, with her educated wisdom, as well as she has. And help has indeed been something they have needed, along with common sense and worldly advice.

Now Dorothy has put pen to paper, as well as voice to tape, and has compiled a fascinating and unforgettable account of the remote spot she knows and loves. The idea of taking a handful of islanders and recording their thoughts and stories in book form gives a far closer and more accurate description than chapters of mere script could do. From what she records one gets a clear and vivid description of what the islanders think and believe — a total insight into what they are like. She has been careful to avoid pitfalls into some of the less flattering aspects of island life — as within its three-mile length a whole world is concentrated, the good and the bad side of human nature; the inner quarrels and hidden antagonisms that exist perfectly naturally in any small community.

As a guest myself on the island for over thirty years, the outcome has been one of devotion to the islanders and a deep understanding of their problems in the face of every type of climatic, as well as governmental, difficulty. My respect for them has never wavered and I know Dorothy shares this sentiment with me. Dorothy is also a superb photographer and her visual as well as her oral interest in the islanders, their lives and their landscape, will be a historical necessity of infinite value in the future.

Perhaps I may be allowed a few comments on reading the exceptional manuscript I have just seen. The 'elephant' washed ashore and finally, when the smell got unbearable, covered with concrete, was, in fact, a sperm whale. Father Eoghan Ó Colm assured me the beast had been an elephant and not a marine creature but, having doubts, I hacked at the concrete till I was able to dig out a large bit of vertebra. I lugged this up to my hut, photographed it and sent a copy to the Natural History Museum in London. The reply was unequivocal — a sperm whale, and quite a rarity in Tory waters. The origin of the name Tory being *tórramh* (funeral), and not the usually accepted theory that the name came from the god Thor or from the 'towers' once existing on the island, is entirely new to me and very convincing — in the last century even, burials of mainlanders from all along the Rosses constantly took place on Arranmore Island, and instead of the line of funeral cars at today's burials, a line of currachs — the leading one carrying the corpse — crossed the channel over to the island graveyard. Similarly the same could well have happened from Falcarragh mainland area out to Tory and its St Colmcille's blessed burial ground. In the case of James Dixon and our after-Mass harbour meeting, when he commented on the picture I was painting, it was his donkey's tail that he made his brushes out of. It was said that in those days there were more donkeys alive on the island than islanders. It was also said that someone had once introduced a goat onto the island and that the donkeys, scenting a rival, had surrounded it and eaten it! In any case the painting brush story is true, as I used to watch Jimmy with fascination when he cut the stiff hairs and made them up into his preferred shape for work.

Whatever is written about Tory Island in the future, and whether Douglas Sealy completes his translation of Father Eoghan Ó Colm's book, *Toraigh na dTonn*, into English, no scholar on this island outpost stranded in the Atlantic will not profit from this masterly contribution; and it comes at the right moment, when it seems the island has become secure from evacuation and that its time immemorial existence is to be respected and continued.

Derek Hill

Preface

On a sunny morning in the early spring of 1982, I stood on the pier of the tiny harbour of Bunbeg, my suitcase beside me, and looked with interest at the fishing trawler *Floredge* tied up to a bollard a couple of feet away. I had been dropped off here by the local taxi and, at that moment, there was no one else to be seen. In a few minutes, however, a man appeared from a small shed near by and walked over to me.

'Are you going to Tory, then?' he asked.

'Yes,' I replied, 'and it's a lovely morning.'

The mate, as he turned out to be, did not acknowledge the beauty of the day. Jerking his head in the direction of the *Floredge*, he said, 'She heaves a bit. You'll probably be sick.' After which pronouncement he stepped onto the trawler's deck and disappeared into the wheelhouse. Soon the skipper, Teddy Doherty, appeared and we were off: half an hour down the protected channel to Bloody Foreland and then out to the open sea and the rough currents of Tory Sound. If I had not taken a precautionary anti-seasickness pill before leaving the hotel, the mate's prophecy would have been fulfilled. As it was, my stomach and I were thankful to reach Tory after an hour and a quarter of heaving, and to climb up the steep steps of the pier at Camusmore, where Patsy Dan Rodgers was waiting to greet me.

I had first set foot on Tory the year before, when a friend and I rented a half-decker at Magheraroarty for the nine-mile trip to the island. Our time was limited to two hours, due to weather and tide, but I did, by chance, meet Patsy Dan and bought one of his paintings. After corresponding with him for several months, I knew that I would surely go back to his 'beautiful island'. On this second trip I was alone, and I had arranged to spend two weeks with Eilish and Eamonn Rodgers. Their house was the only lodging open at all times, and was used mainly by workmen from Donegal County Council. Very few visitors came to Tory in those days and hardly any stayed overnight because of the uncertainty of the return to the mainland. The *Floredge*, bringing the mails, as well as supplies from the shop in Bunbeg, sailed only on Tuesdays and Fridays and, after accomplishing her mission, left as quickly as possible. If the sea was high, she would not come at all, due partly to the difficulty of coming alongside the unprotected pier.

Since that visit, I have returned each year for varying lengths of time and in various seasons, including a few rough weeks one January. For the first ten years, the *Floredge* was my main means of transportation. And for these ten years, Tory remained virtually unchanged – quiet and remarkably isolated, even in summer.

In 1993, after fourteen years of faithful service, the ageing trawler owned by Patrick Doherty (Teddy's brother) was replaced by the *Tor Mór*, a sleek, fast vessel with a cabin and seats outside at the stern for passengers on a fair crossing. It was the new ferry, carrying the mail year round and making three trips a day, every day, from Bunbeg and Magheraroarty during the season (mid-May to mid-September) that was responsible for the many changes that have taken place on the island in the past five years. Now, at last, it is a simple matter to reach the island in good weather. In the summer holidays, people from all over Ireland and some Europeans too have taken advantage of the easy access. Patsy Dan tells me that approximately eight thousand visitors have come each season.

As a result, in addition to Eilish Rodgers' house, there are now several accredited B&Bs available. Four years ago, Patrick and Bernadette Doohan, from East Town, opened their fourteen-room hotel (each room has its private bath) with a dining room and, of course, a bar. It is on the site of the old Ward's hotel next to the wall of the churchyard and, in colour and line, blends well with the adjoining buildings. A small craft shop, with a tea room above it, has opened, and the café, near the community hall, built a year or two before the arival of the *Tor Mór*, is busier than ever. Five years ago, Derek Hill (who has done so much for the island) and I bought Grace Dixon's small house, which has been made into a gallery. The simplicity of its white-washed walls are a perfect setting for the primitive works of Patsy Dan Rodgers,

Anton Meenan, Ruairí Rodgers and Michael Finbar Rodgers. A short walk from the pier, it has many visitors who frequently buy paintings.

A very new addition to the island are about a half-dozen Land Rovers. I complain that walking the road to the East is like walking on a California freeway, but they are useful in many ways, as is the little bus that brings the older people from East to West for mass on Sundays and to the post office for mail and pension cheques. (The inhabitants of East Town are proud of the fact that the visitors seldom walk that far, so their peace and quiet are as yet undisturbed.)

Last but not least – after so many years of discussion and promises that no one thought it would ever happen – the harbour is being deepened and an elbow built at the end of the pier to give it protection. When it is finished, Tory half-deckers will be able to lie at anchor safely and the ferry can tie up at the steps even in quite rough weather. It will take a few more years to finish, as work can be done only when the tide is fully out. But it is on its way, even though some of the older fishermen say that it has come twenty years too late.

The great benefit of the new ferry is that the sense of often helpless isolation has mostly disappeared. The island women, in particular, can now go to the mainland in the season, to shop, or to take a child to the clinic in Letterkenny, and be certain of their return the same day. The painters can get necessary supplies when needed. To the delight of the young people, the summer visitors have been a reason for almost nightly *céilís* at the club and musical evenings in the bar of the hotel. In winter, the ferry makes the mail runs when possible and in addition, as it has done for the past ten or twelve years, a helicopter provided by Údarás na Gaeltachta comes twice a month between December and March to take people to the mainland for the day. Sometimes, when there has been a spell of very bad weather, it will make a few extra trips.

Some of the older people do not like the changes. They feel there are too many visitors and too much busyness. I must admit that, selfishly, I also much preferred the peace and isolation I found on my early visits, though I would feel differently, I'm sure, if I had to live on the island all year round. Tory is no longer the legendary, almost mythical place it once was, though it manages to keep its unique charm.

Some visitors wander as far as the lighthouse to the west or eastwards towards Portadoon and experience the island's special beauty. For Tory does have its own special beauty. In late spring and summer, pink thrift blooms among the cliffs and rocks; campion and the bright yellow petals of a plant whose name I do not know grow on banks near the sea. Buttercups and small white daisies liven the fields and roadsides, and other wild flowers, delicate and sturdy, surprise the eye. Fluffy tufts of bog cotton turn pockets of wet bogland into white pools above which the black and white oystercatchers circle, calling anxiously; and gulls nest on the eastern cliffs, looking 'like spectators in the boxes of a theatre', to quote Alfred McFarland. The engaging puffins, with their clown faces, pop in and out of their cliff burrows and fly low over the sea with flittering wings. Friendly little brown birds of some sort are seldom far away when one takes a walk; and the corncrake, now an endangered species, runs on long legs in the meadows and gardens, making its invisible presence known only by its rasping 'crex, crex'. Once, on a cold, grey day, I saw a vagrant American oriole alight for a moment on a grey stone wall before disappearing in a brilliant flash of colour.

In autumn, the rough tussocks of heather dotting the waste land, or following the ruins of ancient stone walls, come into their own, purple and sweet scented. The meadows lose some of their fresh green but other fields take on a tint of bronze. Winter, with its depressingly short daytime hours, its frequent gales and its pervasive greyness, is cruel. But for me, who need not live through its unforgiving harshness year after year, there is beauty in the immense Atlantic rollers breaking in long lines on the reefs near the lighthouse, with spray, thick as mist, rising above their crests. Nowhere on the island is one out of sight of the sea. Northwards it stretches unbroken to the horizon; to the south it is edged by the mainland. The outline of the mainland coast, called 'the country' by the islanders, is shaded from grey to deep blue and pale green, depending on the light, and is always a part of the landscape: Horn Head to the east, then flat-topped Muckish Mountain, the hills of Bloody Foreland and, to the west, the pointed peak of Errigal. It is beautiful in all seasons and at all times looks deceptively near.

It was during 1981, the year in which I set foot upon Tory for the first time, that I also discovered the uses of a tape recorder. When I returned in 1982 I began experimenting with it by taping songs and dances. The islanders are noted for their great love of music and the local musicians include several accordion players, a fiddler and various men and women with fine *a capella* voices. I heard both modern and traditional songs and ballads, some of the latter quite different from what many think of as Irish music. For, according to an old friend, a musician who specialises in the traditional songs, 'Irish music owes much of its richness and unexpected changes of mood to the fact that a very great number of airs are written in modes rather than the more modern keys.' A few of the ballads had been written on Tory by the grandfathers of those who sang them for me, which made them of special interest. During this visit I also taped some reels and country dances at the Sunday night *céilí,* as well as a few stories told to me by Pádraig Óg Rodgers.

Because of these very pleasant experiences, I decided that the next time I was on Tory I would ask a few more of the older men and women to tell me something about their lives and those of their parents; perhaps some fairy stories and legends as well. Those I approached were happy to do this and seemed to enjoy the resulting conversations, for our sessions were always more social than serious. I think the fact that I came to Tory with no professional purpose, and continued to come out of friendship and a concern for the problems of the island, accounts for whatever interest or value the stories may have. It certainly accounts for their informality. So began my first attempt at collecting oral history *(béaloideas* in Irish; literally, mouth learning), without the slightest thought of possible publication. I decided, however, once I realised that I was accumulating quite a few stories, that I would have them typed and bound privately and give them to the small library in the Tory schoolhouse. The advent on the island of twenty-four hour electricity in 1981 — and therefore television — had meant the death of the old-fashioned custom of story-telling.

Transcribing the tapes over the following several years was another new experience, somewhat difficult at first but becoming easier as my ear grew more attuned to Tory voices and words. I listened to the tapes many times to make sure that my renditions were correct and when the first few transcriptions were typed I looked them over eagerly. The stories moved neatly across the pages with what I had thought was the appropriate punctuation, the correct paragraphs, but to my dismay there was something missing. I realised suddenly that their very tidiness obscured the cadence, the sense of a story told. There were no pauses, no emphases, no silences. I was not quite sure what to do about it.

In November 1985, I was taken by friends to a lecture given by Professor Henry Glassie (Professor of Folklore at the Folklore Institute, Indiana University, Bloomington, and author, among other books, of *Passing the Time in Ballymenone*). I had an opportunity to speak to him briefly and told him about my collection, and that I could not think of how to put them on paper so that the cadence would be preserved. 'I could show you how to do that in ten minutes,' he offered generously, 'but really what you must do is *listen* to the *silences*.' I did not happen to see him again. Two months later, in a summerhouse in a Jamaican garden, surrounded by sun-lit tropical flowers and the whirr of hummingbirds' wings, I sat down with tapes, pencil and paper, put on my earphones and began to listen with a different ear to the familiar Tory voices — and to the silences.

It was only after I had redone the tapes, hearing them in a different way, and with the encouragement of several friends, to whom I had shown a small section of my endeavours, that I began to weave stories, personal experiences and some gentle research into a book. Two excellent books have already been written about the island. The first of these is Fr Eoghan Ó Colm's *Toraigh na dTonn* (Tory of the Waves), published in 1971 (and yet to be translated into English). Fr Ó Colm was the island curate from 1956 to 1962. During these six years, he lived and worked with the Tory people, helping them in the fields, hearing their confessions, learning their ways and listening to their stories. He was their friend as well as their priest. The second book is *The Tory Islanders: A People of the Celtic Fringe* (Cambridge, 1978) by Robin Fox, Professor of Anthropology at Rutgers University, New Jersey. In the author's own words, '... I was in Donegal thinking about studying bilingualism. I hopped aboard a boat simply because it was going, and Tory, like Everest, was there. That was in 1960.' After much research and delay, the book was published in 1978, and the result was a fascinating study of a unique people. The inhabitants of an island so long isolated must, of necessity, be resilient and even in these days fairly independent. The people of Tory are complex, reserved and devoutly Roman Catholic, although their roots seem, at times, still firmly planted in pagan soil; their traditions, customs and superstitions are intricate. Although Fr Ó Colm and Professor Fox come from different cultural and intellectual backgrounds, they both clearly show affection and respect for those about whom they wrote.

Stories from Tory Island is also written with affection and respect. Its purpose is the telling of some island tales. Although it consists mainly of island tales, this book is more than just a collection of folklore. Having spent a total of seven months on Tory, from 1982 to 1988 in various seasons of the year, it is my recognition of an island and its people. It is as well an appreciation of many happy days in all weathers, of meeting and making friends, of companionship and solitude, of windswept beauty, of welcomes and farewells. The stories told to me by the storytellers could stand on their own, but I have indulged myself by adding to them some excerpts from the writings of several nineteenth-century travellers and antiquaries, chosen as much for their delightful literary style as for their historical context. Some kind friends provided me with photocopies of excerpts from historians of an earlier period. Among these is Manus O'Donnell, whose facts were not always accurate, at least in the opinion of Dr Edward Maguire. After quoting from 'the legendary account of the fates and fortunes of the Tory Columban monastery', Maguire wrote chidingly, 'Manus

O'Donnell, inexact as elsewhere in his chronology. . .' I am sure that I, too, would be sternly corrected by the reverend doctor for inexactness in chronology while trying to combine legend and history. Listening to the stories told to me by the islanders, from the days of the wicked Balor and the good St Colmcille to the days of their own fathers and grandfathers, it often seemed as though but a short period had elapsed between the two. And it was always evident from the names given to every tor, cleft, meadow and rock on the island, that legend and local history, myth and reality continue to be timelessly interwoven.

Originally I transcribed the tapes word for word, but, in the interest of making the stories easier to read and understand, I have edited them to a certain extent without, I hope, the loss of their original flavour. I have omitted some repetitive passages, added a verb here or a noun there for clarity, and used the correct pronouns when necessary as the typically indiscriminate use of 'he', 'she' and 'it' is confusing. I have also omitted some stories as being too personal. Although the islanders are remarkably articulate in English, considering the fact that less than fifty years ago few spoke English at all, Irish is their first language; therefore it must be remembered that these stories are really translations and so lack the easy flow and special idiom of their native tongue. As you read, please keep in mind the Tory dictum 'time enough'. And when there seems to be a pause, a silence, listen for the ticking of a wall clock, the purr of a cat on a warm hearth, a neighbour's footsteps at the door, the clink of fire-tongs adding another sod to the fire. Above all, be aware of the sea that surrounds you. It may not always be audible but it is omnipresent.

Since this book was first published, gentle Madge Rodgers has died, and so has Dónal Doohan. Dónal became ill and was taken to Letterkenny hospital shortly after one of my visits. I was told that he had a 'blockage' but refused to be operated upon. To everyone's surprise, including the doctors', he recovered. He was then sent to the old people's home in Falcarragh. When I heard this I was sad, for I was sure that he would be dead in six months, homesick for Tory and its fresh sea air. I could not have been more wrong. He thrived on the warmth and companionship in the small, well-run institution. For three or four years before his death, I went to see him on my way in to Tory and on my return.

On one visit I told him of the terrible weather on the island, two weeks of rain and occasional gale force winds. He smiled. 'In here,' he said, 'it is always summer.' The last time I saw him he was sleeping, tucked snugly in blankets in his bed by the window. He looked very small and frail. When I woke him gently, his pale blue eyes looked at me for a moment without recognition. Then he smiled and said: 'It's you, Dorrikin.' He was happy to see me, and I sat with him for quite a while, holding his hand.

From mid-May to mid-September, Tory may be a hive of activity but in winter the island is once more *creig i lár na farraige, i measc éanacha na mbeann* (a rock in the middle of the sea, amongst the birds of the cliffs). When the gales blow and the sea is high, and the great breakers near the lighthouse roll in clouds of spray, and the waves crash over the pier at Camusmore, Tory is as isolated as it ever was. That will never change. In spite of all that has taken place, Patsy Dan could still write to me, as he did some years ago, 'tonight again a tough night, since the past few weeks very tough weather indeed. It's been hellish altogether... There'll be no trawler in tomorrow. It's that rough even the Queen Mary couldn't make it in to Tory.'

Introduction

Tory Island lies nine miles out in the North Atlantic off Bloody Foreland on the north-west coast of Co Donegal. On a grey day it is the colour of charcoal against the grey sky; when the sun is bright, and the sea a deep blue, it is sometimes opalescent, sometimes shadowed in sapphire and golden brown. It appears always as a castellated mirage on the horizon

Over the years Tory has been described as the most isolated, the most desolate, the most windswept of any of the Irish islands. Winter is not the only season when the winds blow fiercely. Alfred McFarland who visited Tory in August 1849 wrote, in *Hours in Vacation* (Dublin, 1853), of the fury of the tides and the violence of the gales. While waiting on the mainland at Falcarragh for the packet that was to take him to the island, he met a 'worthy Doctor and Reverend priest' who had been on Tory for several days, 'held in durance sad by contrary winds'. Having insisted that they be taken back to the mainland in spite of continuing strong winds and rough seas, 'their boat was driven from its course, and beaten about for hours, till at last they reached the shore, drenched to the skin and numbed with cold — the Doctor protesting that the place must have been the last which God made; and his Reverence holding that it could not belong to his parish at least.'

There is not a tree on Tory. The central part of the island is green, where the fields and meadows lie at the approaches to the northern tors of Mearnaid, Miodhaird and Moraid; at the eastern and western ends there are large areas of waste land. Here, centuries of turf-cutting have left a legacy of brown, gravelly soil and bog dotted with low tussocks of rough heather and, scattered between these, a veritable moonscape of white and grey stones.

To the north, rugged cliffs of quartzite, sandstone and red granite protect the community, in some measure, from the battering of the winter gales. To the south, the land slopes gently to the sea and here, separated by three-quarters of a mile of narrow bumpy road, are the two towns, or villages. West Town, the larger of the two, holds the principal buildings: the church, the parochial house, the school, the post office with the public telephone, the dispensary, two shops, the community hall and most of the antiquities. East Town has a superb view of Horn Head and the mountains of Muckish and Errigal on the mainland, as well as a shop and now a telephone. Fields and meadows that once produced oats, corn and barley as well as potatoes are spread around the two villages; they are now used mainly for hay and as grazing for the few sheep and cattle and the retired donkeys.

At the western tip of the island stands the lighthouse, which was built in 1832 and is ninety feet high, with walls seven feet thick at the base. It was on the rocks below that the British frigate HMS *Wasp* was wrecked in 1884 on her way to collect, by force, rates and rents owed to the absentee landlord, Benjamin St John Baptist Joule, a businessman from Manchester. Joule had purchased Tory Island along with some mainland property for £6500 in 1861, but he could collect hardly any rent, and none at all after 1872. The islanders believed, with good reason, that the *Wasp* was coming to evict them, for in those days the tenants of many Irish islands were removed from their homes for nonpayment of even the smallest rents. Island tradition has it that she was wrecked due to the efficient use of the Tory cursing stone.

The cliffs along the north coast are penetrated deeply by inlets, or clefts *(scoilteanna)*. To the east of the lighthouse, not far from the little Protestant graveyard, where some of HMS *Wasp*'s crew is buried, is Scoilt an Mhuiriseáin. Onto its stony beach, in the time of St Colmcille, there drifted a boat carrying seven people. Dr Edward Maguire quotes Manus O'Donnell, the sixteenth-century author of *The Life of St Columba*: 'The fame of his [St Colmcille's] wisdom, his knowledge, his faith, his piety, had gone forth throughout the entire world, and the holy children of the King of India had conceived love for him on account of the rumours .. there were six sons (of them) and one sister.' The children set sail in search of him and were not heard from for a long time, until they finally reached the north-west coast of Tory. 'And on their coming to land, they died in consequence of the fatigue of the sea and of the ocean.' They were brought across the island and buried together at a place on the edge of what is now West Town, where the foundations of one of St Colmcille's little chapels are still visible. But for three mornings in a row, the body of the woman was found lying on top of the grave, so she was buried separately and from then on rested peacefully; Alfred McFarland believed that the seven were Scandinavian royalty; T J Westropp stated in the *Antiquarian Handbook Series* in 1905 that they were Hollanders. Dan Rodgers of Tory Island says the islanders thought the woman might have been a saint. And it is from the grave site of the 'saint' that the eldest of the Duggan clan retains the prerogative given to him by St Colmcille to lift 'holy clay', which has the power not only to banish rats, but to protect fishermen from the dangers of the sea.

Beyond Scoilt an Mhuiriseáin and a little farther to the east is Greenport (Poirtín Ghlais) which, as it faces north, is of no use as shelter for boats in the winter months. Balor, the legendary Fomorian pirate and ruler of Tory in ancient times, landed in this small cove after stealing the magic cow from Gabhan, the smith who had his forge on the mainland at Drumnatinny. This white milch cow, called *glas gaibhlinn,* was, according to Rev J McDevitt in *The Donegal Highlands* (Dublin, 1866), 'so lactiferous as to be greatly coveted by the neighbours', and the smith seldom let go of her halter by day and was careful to tie her securely at night. Balor desired her greatly and one day, assuming the guise of a red-haired little boy, he tricked Gabhan into letting him hold her halter while the smith went into the forge to settle an argument. As soon as the smith was out of sight, Balor ran off with the cow and, after stopping for a short rest on the nearby island of Inishbofin, came to Greenport and dragged his prize up the beach by the tail. Why was this famous cow called *glas* (green, or grey) when she was, from all accounts, white? The answer, perhaps, is in a book called *Mearing Stones: Leaves from my Note-book on Tramp in Donegal* by Joseph Campbell (Dublin,

1911). On one of his walks, Campbell noticed an exceptionally green field and asked the farmer if there was water near it. The man replied that a stream did run through it, but that the *glas gaibhlinn* also slept there. He explained further, "'It's a magic cow the old people'll tell you of," says he, "that could never be milked at one milking, or at seven milkings, for that," says he. "Any field that's greener than another field, or any bit of land that's richer than another bit, they say *glas gaibhlinn* sleeps in it," says he. "It's a freet, but it's true!'"

To the south-east of the lighthouse is Camas Beag (Little Bay), which opens into the Camas Mór (Big Bay, now called Camusmore). Here, at West Town, is the long pier built in 1903 by the Congested Districts Board, a government body responsible for roads, housing and harbours. The pier offers little protection from the winds, but Séamus Ward persuaded the authorities, so it is said, to put it at this location because of its proximity to his shop and licensed public house. At the head of the nearby slip, down which all Tory boats are launched for the fishing season and for trips to the mainland during spells of good weather, is the Tau-shaped cross, also known to antiquaries as St Andrew's cross, or the Egyptian cross. Made of thick mica slate, it stands six feet high and for many years has been embedded in a base of stone and cement. There is only one other like it in Ireland, the smaller, but better known, cross at Kilnaboy, Co Clare. This relic of the time of Colmcille has always been important to the islanders, especially to the men who, in small frail currachs, made their living from the sea and prayed, as they passed the cross on their way to their boats, for a safe return.

Further on, below East Town, is the sandy, gently sloping beach of Port Deilg (Port of the Pin). According to folklore, when Balor — driven by a prophecy that he would be slain by his own grandson — found that his daughter had borne triplets, he sent the babies off as quickly as possible, rolled up in a sheet fastened by a pin, with orders that they be thrown into a certain whirlpool. On the way, however, the pin fell out of the sheet and the three dropped into a small harbour. Two drowned, but Lugh, Balor's grandson, was rescued by a banshee. The scalloped harbour from which Lugh was saved has been called Port Deilg to this day. Tory islander Seán Rodgers gives a local version of the story: A long time ago, when bodies were brought in to the island to be buried, they arrived at Port Deilg in unvarnished coffins covered with white sheets. Before the coffins were carried to the old graveyard at West Town, the sheets were removed, and the pins that had held them together were thrown into the sea.

At the far eastern end of the island where, at the approach to the massive cliffs of Dún Balor and Tor Mór, only about thirty yards separate the north and south coasts, is Portadoon or Port an Dúin (Port of the Fort). A concrete pier hugs the western side and, to the north, there is a beach of pretty pink and grey stones. On a sunny day, with the tide whispering gently on the strand, it is difficult to imagine that it was in this peaceful place that in pre-Christian times the legendary Nemedians and Fomorians fought so bitterly that the sea beyond the pink and grey stones was stained red with their blood.

Short history

In spite of its distance from the mainland, its hostile environment and its small size (two and a half miles long, three-quarters of a mile wide), Tory has been inhabited for centuries and, according to Robin Fox in *The Tory Islanders: A People of the Celtic Fringe* (Cambridge, 1978), is one of the earliest places mentioned by the bards. In pre-Christian times it was occupied by the legendary Nemedians, said to have come to Ireland from Scythia. Later came the equally legendary Fomorians (literally, giants or pirates), described by John O'Donovan in *Letters Containing Information Relative to the Antiquities of the County of Donegal* (Ordnance Survey of Ireland, 1834), as 'African Mariners... who are supposed, not improbably, to have been Carthaginian traders'. Traders or pirates, they roved and raided the Irish coasts and oppressed the Nemedians with cruel taxes, including the demand that two-thirds of the Nemedian children born each year be given over to them. Periodic and savage battles were fought between the two tribes and of one of these struggles, which took place at Portadoon on Tory, O'Donovan writes: 'In the book of St Caillin, it is stated that the Nemedians and Fomorians fought on the strand so furiously that they felt not the tide flowing around them, and that they continued the fight until they were swept away by the sea.'

From these contentious times and throughout its history, Tory has had an assortment of uncrowned 'kings'. One of the first of these was the Fomorian Conán. As related in ancient manuscripts, he built a tower on the island from which he made frequent sorties to plunder the mainland, and soon Tor Inis (Island of the Tower), became well known. The bardic poets wrote of Conán and his tower and of how the Nemedians became so outraged by defeats and oppression at the hands of the 'African Mariners' that they raised an army. Alfred McFarland's book gives a translation of a tenth-century poem: 'Sixty thousand of brave men /valiant forces both by land and sea/was the number of the army which marched forth/of the Nemedians to destroy The Tower.' Having killed the 'king' and levelled his tower, they regained possession of their isolated stronghold, but they did not keep it for long, at least as one counted time those thousands of years ago, and another Fomorian seized power.

This new 'king' was Balor of the Evil Eye, Balor of the Mighty Blows, in Celtic mythology the demon of night. The tales of his deeds and misdeeds were so many and so outrageous that his fame quickly eclipsed that of Conán. He, too, made Tory his headquarters. He terrified the islanders, took food from them without recompense and robbed the passing ships so successfully that, according to an old Tory man, he was able to bury nine tons of bars of gold somewhere near his fort, Dún Balor, on the eastern end of the island. Balor's 'prison' lies not far from the fort, in a cleft at the base of Tor Mór. It was here, because of the aforementioned prophecy, that Balor held captive for many years his only daughter, Ethnea (moon goddess), guarded by twelve matrons whose sole concern was to keep her unaware of the existence of men. Despite her father's precautions Ethnea's son, Lugh (sun god), eventually fulfilled the prophecy by killing his grandfather in a battle between the Fomorians and the Tuatha Dé Danaan (peoples of the goddess Danu — pre-Christian deities of day, fertility, goodness and wisdom).

Introduction xxvii

Needless to say, the stories about Balor are interpreted quite differently by the islanders than by students of mythology. But mythical or not, to the Tory people Balor plays as human and important a role as any in the long and turbulent history of the island.

Hundreds of years passed and spoken legend became written history. In the sixth century rulers of a different persuasion took charge of Tory. St Colmcille (literally, dove of the church) brought Christianity to the island and banished the pagans forever. The 'passionate pigeon', as the nineteenth-century Protestant cleric Caesar Otway referred to him as in *Sketches in Ireland* (Dublin, 1827), was born to a noble family at Gartan in Co Donegal in AD 521, and played an important role in the history of Tory where relics of his presence and influence still remain. Among the versions given as to why and how he came to Tory, Robin Fox recounts that, as the result of a mystical vision, Colmcille chose Tory for the site of a monastic settlement. Having prevailed in a dispute with rivals, who were competing with him for the honour of bringing the 'true faith' to this desolate spot, 'his position as saint of saints in Ireland was established when God opened the waters of Tory Sound for him and he walked across to the island.'

Local folklore tells a different story: Colmcille wished to build a monastery on Tory, not only to bring Christianity to its pagan inhabitants, but also because of its isolated situation, which made it an ideal place for quiet contemplation. With two others of like mind, St Finian and St Begley, he climbed to the top of a hill above the townland of Magheraroarty, a hill still known as Cnoc na Naomh (Hill of the Saints). From here Tory can be seen clearly — a long, thin, grey line on the horizon. It was decided that each would throw his crosier in the direction of the island; the one whose crosier reached it would go there and fulfil his wish. One by one, Finian and Begley threw their crosiers and prayed, 'With my help and the help of God, may this crosier reach Tory. Colmcille, however, by invoking God's name at the beginning of the prayer, succeeded where the others had failed. His crosier turned into a javelin and flew swiftly to Tory, and a large, crater-like hollow near the north-eastern cliffs is said to be the place where it landed. He then crossed Tory Sound in a currach.

Colmcille built a church and seven small chapels, and possibly the *cloigtheach* (belfry or round tower). McFarland wrote concerning the church, 'The present ruin is still called his Cathedral church. It resembles a cross in shape, and seems to have preserved a vigorous existence until the close of the sixteenth century, when it was sacked, but most of its walls are still standing.' In 1845, Edmund Getty, accompanied by two friends, explored Tory, a trip that resulted in his account, 'The Island of Tory; Its History and Antiquities', published in 1853 in *The Ulster Journal of Archaeology*. A sketch by Getty shows the ruins of 'the eastern arched gateway of the Abbey enclosure', situated between the round tower and the Tau cross. The tower, made roofless by a storm many years ago, still stands but only the foundations of one of the small chapels are now visible.

St Ernan followed Colmcille about a century later and for twenty years was abbot of the monastery. In his *History of the Diocese of Raphoe* (Dublin, 1920) Dr Edward Maguire suggests that St Ernan enlarged the building area as the community grew and that he repaired the ravages resulting from the frequent attacks by the predatory fleets of the time. In fact, according to Dr Maguire, 'The illustrious St Ernan renewed the face of the entire island, realising the grand ideal of the great Columba, and under his blessed rule, Tory attained to the zenith of its fame.' St Ernan, in turn, was followed by the Erenachs, archdeacons or church wardens, who looked after the church property for the bishop of Raphoe, within whose parish of Kilmacrennan Tory lay. From the eleventh to the seventeenth century, and perhaps beyond, these trustees paid the bishop seven shillings a year and, among other items, a goodly supply of poteen (illegal whiskey). Dr Maguire wrote, 'Poteen making was a long established and lucrative industry of the islanders, and as the Bishop was entitled to receive "fortie tertian madders of maulte for every balliboe inhabited", he would never dream of crippling the resources of production by threats of censures or "reservations".'

According to Robin Fox, after the Erenachs followed 'the "royal" family of Brehons, the lawgivers'; if there were other rulers of Tory — either sinners or saints — I am not aware of them until, in the middle of the nineteenth century, a man called Paddy Heggarty became known as 'king'. E Estyn Evans wrote in *Irish Heritage* (Dundalk, 1942): 'It was formerly the task of an appointed leader in a townland or group of townlands to see that customs were observed, to arrange the casting of lots in re-allotting of strips, and so on. Probably we should see in the "king", not long ago recognised as a leader in such communities as Rathlin [Island] and Tory, a relic of this custom.' Literacy was, of course, the major requisite for the position.

Paddy Heggarty, though not island-born (he is said to have come originally from Co Sligo) was, for a time, the schoolmaster on Tory. He was, indeed, literate and very clever with the written word. He was also a dwarf, standing, from all accounts, only four feet tall. Alfred McFarland visited 'Paddy Heggarty, alias Harrison' who at that time was living in the 'Cottage' at the east end, a somewhat cluttered establishment that seemed to have been used as an early type of bed-and-breakfast. (It was enlarged and improved later and in 1854 a notice was placed in the *Derry Journal* by 'Patrick Herison, King of Tory, informing the public that his 'hotel' was open.) McFarland described him as being about forty years old, with a well-shaped head, intelligent features and thick, curly, black hair. Eventually, Heggarty had a falling-out with the Tory priest and moved to Rathlin Island where, no doubt in righteous protest, he became a Protestant. Though he died on Rathlin, he is buried in Gortahork, Co Donegal, but outside the walls of the graveyard, as befitted a Protestant.

When Paddy Heggarty left Tory, Niall Ward became the prominent figure on the island, although he was not actually referred to as 'king'. He came from Burtonport, a fishing village on the mainland and, having spent some time on Tory as a lighthouse keeper, married a Tory woman. He bought land and built a house at the east side of West Town, described by Pádraig Óg Rodgers as 'a lovely residential place for visitors, the same as a hotel'. His son Séamus followed him and, before the turn of the century, made the house into a real hotel with a public house and shop attached. Over the years several well-known people stayed there, including Sir Roger Casement, an ardent Irish nationalist, who was hanged by the British in 1916. Séamus himself had been a member of the Gaelic League, an organisation to promote Irish culture, and was a champion stepdancer. The islanders considered him to be 'a powerful strong man' and he was referred to locally as the 'king'. By the time Séamus left Tory to live on the mainland, Pádraig Óg Rodgers, another man clever with words, had already given up fishing to 'use the pen'. A man with the ability to write skilfully and clearly and to interpret legal documents was always of particular value to the island, especially during the absence of a priest. The people chose Pádraig as their next 'king', which he remained until his death in 1988.

The real ruler of the island, however, has been, and continues to be, the ever unpredictable sea. It is the most important factor in the lives of the Tory people. Since transportation to and from the island is still mainly by boat, high seas, even in the summer, make communication with the mainland difficult; when the winter gales blow, Tory is often isolated for as long as two or three weeks at a time. So the island people and those who choose to visit them, like McFarland's 'worthy Doctor and Reverend priest', must live as always dependent upon the moods of wind and waves.

William Harkin, a fellow of the Royal Society of Antiquarians, Ireland, made a trip to Tory in 1892 and described in *Scenery and Antiquities of North-West Donegal* (Derry, 1893) how he and his friends 'were landed on the far-famed "Iona of Donegal"'. Samuel Bayne, travelling from New York to Derry in 1902 on the new twin-screw steamer SS *Columbia* of the Anchor Line, wrote in *On an Irish Jaunting Car through Donegal and Connemara* (New York and London, 1902) of sighting Tory: 'It has been called "the Sentinel of the Atlantic" and it is well named, being the first land one sees when nearing Ireland.'

There is a variety of opinion as to the derivation of the name Tory, or Torry. For indeed, as Alfred McFarland noted, 'What is an Irish island without a name, and one about which the antiquarians will never agree?' McFarland himself gives the general version that it was called Tor Inis (Island of the Tower);

maybe it was just Torach (Towery), or perhaps Tor Rí, which could mean the king's (Balor's) rock. He also 'notices the suggestion which ascribes the name of the place to its presenting the appearance, merely, of a number of towers... as viewed from the Cross-roads [Falcarragh]'. Caesar Otway, that adventurous English clergyman, wrote: 'The name of this island is of Runick etymology, and Thor-Eye, now corrupted into Torry, denotes that it was consecrated to Thor, the Scandinavian deity, that presided over stormy and desolate places.' Robin Fox presents the possibility that Oileán Thoraí could be translated as 'Island of the Pirates', *toraí* meaning thief, brigand, or outlaw in Irish. From the late seventeenth century in England, to call a man a Tory — as opposed to Whig — was to compare him to the Papist outlaws of Ireland. Tory politicians, ironically, gave rise to the English conservative party.

But let the scholars and the travellers have their say and turn now to the version that the Tory islanders themselves, the old men particularly, seem to prefer:

Pádraig Óg Rodgers (1984): 'Long ago, I heard from an elderly relative of mine who was a very good Irish scholar too. And he told me long ago, when they were going to bury people that would die on the mainland, that they would come back to Tory Island. And they used to call it in Irish, Tory Island, Oileán Tórramh, the "funerals island".'

And so, as Dónal Doohan, the oldest of the storytellers, would say, 'I will leave it at that. And that's the way it is.'

Dónal Doohan
(b. 1898)

When I began to stay on Tory for three consecutive weeks at a time in 1983, Patsy Dan and Kathleen Rodgers were living in a rented house in West Town. It is situated on the street across from the post office and facing the head of the pier; its central position encouraging people to stop by in the evenings to enjoy its hospitable atmosphere and the good conversation. I went there every evening but was apt to arrive earlier than others who, in true Tory fashion, seldom appeared before eleven. The front door of the house opens into a passage that leads to the stairs and the back kitchen beyond; to the right, as one enters, is the sitting room, somewhat confusingly known on Tory as the 'kitchen', a relic of the days long ago when one room was used for cooking as well as for living and sleeping. Unlike most island houses there was no turf fire in the kitchen; instead, a solid-fuel stove provided much warmth, kept the kettle boiling and dried the nappies (diapers) and other baby clothes that were hung above it. It was a cosy and comfortable place and it was here that I first became aware of Dónal Doohan.

Several times a week I would arrive to find two old men in heavy jerseys and cloth caps sitting side by side on the sofa. One was Johnny Doohan, Kathleen's father, the other was Dónal; they were not related. Johnny was a big man, Dónal small in comparison (he is known as Dónal Beag — Small Dónal). Wisps of yellowed hair escaped from under his ever-present cap and his eyes were blue and remarkably clear for one of eighty-four years. The two men were about the same age and had been good friends all their lives, sharing many memories. Although Johnny was almost blind and both were quite deaf, they were somehow able to communicate, in Irish, without apparent difficulty. I did not have any conversation with Dónal that year for he seemed rather remote, perhaps because of his deafness, but Patsy Dan, I discovered later, had asked him to sing for me, knowing how much I would enjoy it, and Dónal had promised that he would. 'He's a brave singer,' Patsy told me. 'If he can't remember the words, he makes them up as he goes along.' Dónal was going to sing a song called 'McPherson's Wedding', which he had heard long ago in Scotland, but it happened that I left the island before he had a chance to do so. The following year, however, he was able to fulfil his promise. Soon after I arrived on Tory, I went on one of my nightly visits to the Rodgers' and found Dónal, Bridget Doohan (Kathleen's mother) and several other people there already filling the room with a pleasant sound of talk and laughter. In one corner, near the stove, my small 'honorary godson', Seán Dónal, slept in his pram; on the wall above him hung a large poster of Elvis Presley and next to this a Sacred Heart picture that was lit from below by a rose-coloured electric light. Dónal, who had been told that I was coming to hear him sing, was comfortably ensconced on the sofa. When I had checked my tape recorder I went over to sit beside him. After a few words and a nod from me he began to give the introduction, the 'meanings' of the song.

> And McPherson, he was a millionaire. A millionaire.
>
> And he was married late, did ye know, and there was eight hundred at the wedding. Eight hundred. He called everyone in the district to be at the wedding.
>
> And they were making ready for it for a week. Taking in food, drinks. Barrels coming in with wine, stout, beer, whiskey; and it lasted eight days.
>
> Ah, it was great at the finish, the crime start at the finish. They start to fight.
>
> And they were taken away to hospitals; to prison. Guards [policemen] coming in. Detectives coming in.
>
> Ambulance going day and night. Taking them to the hospital.

Breaking their ribs. Breaking their arms. Breaking their legs. Ah, doing everything.

The district stopped. No business.

They made a big song about it and I picked up some of the song.

I'd like to sing it till you hear it — only for the child.

Seán Dónal, in the pram by the stove, had been fussing a little but was now asleep again. Patsy Dan reassured Dónal. 'Oh, it's all right, it's OK. Sing away, *a thaisce.*'

'I never sing sitting,' said Dónal firmly, 'I wouldn't sing right.'

Patsy went over to the sofa and, getting a firm grip on the old man's arm, heaved him out of its depths. Once on his feet, Dónal announced, 'I was telling you before about the reason for the song. And here's the beginning now.' He cleared his throat. Standing as erect as a soldier on review, arms tight against his sides, he began to sing.

By yon bonnie banks and by yon bonnie braes
Oh, the sun shines bright on Loch Lomond,
And for I and my true love will never meet again
On the bonnie, bonnie banks of Loch Lomond.

The song was the traditional rendition of 'Loch Lomond', but with the following verse added before the final refrain. Dónal warned us: 'And here's the trouble now! The trouble now at the wedding!'

Ohhh, the doctors will come the high road,
And the nurses will come the low road,
And the ambulance will go through the gloaming.
It was here that there was sin, it was a mortal sin,
That was here at the weddin'-of-McPherson-in-the-gloamin'.

Dónal then swung briskly into the refrain:

*And you'll take the high road and I will take the low road
And I will be in Scotland before you,
For I and my true love will never meet again
On the bonnie, bonnie banks of Loch Lomond.*

When the song was finished Dónal sat down happily while the audience cheered, laughed and clapped. Patsy Dan was delighted. 'Now! Fair play to ye, fair play to ye. It's years ago, many years ago that I heard you singing.'

'Oh, did ye hear me?'

'Yes,' said Patsy, 'in the schoolhouse. Fair play to ye. Great memory.'

Dónal turned to me. 'I heard that the time you were here before, that you went away; and I promised you that I was coming here to sing you a song. I was sorry when I heard in the morning "She's away."'

Patsy Dan shouted in his ear, 'Well, you're stand to your promise tonight!'

'Oh, aye, aye. I will sing a couple of ones before you go; I had a lot if I can catch them. I will think tonight when I go to bed. And that's the time I think. I will think on them. Aye.'

* * *

From this time on I visited Dónal frequently. He loves company and, to encourage my visits, searched his mind diligently for songs to sing or stories to tell 'Dorikin', as he calls me. Usually I would find him at home sitting by the hearth in the kitchen, his old grey and white cat on his knee. The room is sparsely furnished: worn linoleum on the floor, a small double-burner gas stove in one corner, a table by the window, a bench placed against the back wall, a cupboard and two chairs. There is a picture of the Sacred Heart, coloured photographs of the Pope and of President John F Kennedy, and a large, brown, battery-run clock hangs above the chair in which he always sits. The chair faces the window that looks out on the street and Dónal keeps a keen eye on all the passers-by. If, on my way for a walk or to visit someone else, I did not have time to stop in, I would slip around the house by the eastern gable-end where there is no window so that he would not see me and be disappointed. Once I entered his room and sat down for a while it was difficult to leave. He would clutch at my sleeve as I got up from my chair, follow me to the door and try with promises of yet another story to make me stay a little longer. Finally, I was forced to give him an ultimatum: either I would come for a full hour every few days, or for half an hour every day. He chose the latter and from then on, as I walked to the door and turned to say a final goodbye, he would remain in his chair, smiling and chuckling loudly.

I learned quickly that Dónal is a 'brave' storyteller indeed, his poetic licence boundless. No gale blew less than ninety to a hundred miles an hour; a whale swallowed whole 'a skiff with eight of crew'; some of the *slua sí* (fairy host) carried 'guns and ammunition. — well armed'. What is sadly missing from the written page is his dramatic use of facial expressions and body movements to illustrate the stories. The *cú nimhe* (poison hound) of the pagans glares with a look that kills; the crew of a boat rows desperately, struggling against heavy seas, and Dónal rows with them: 'When the big wave comes — backing, backing. When the wave will go down, pull now away again, away again!' And the hay mice, with their little pointy noses, scuttle in the walls and the thatch of his grandmother's house as Dónal's fingers scramble in the air. He gives a great performance.

From my conversations with Dónal and from bits of information given to me by Patsy Dan, I learned a good bit about the old man's life. He was born in 1898 in a thatched house, the youngest of ten children, five boys and five girls. One of his earliest memories is lying in bed between his mother and father, watching the blazing turf fire and seeing the horse standing at one side of the hearth and the cow lying down at the other. 'The cattle was in that time, the old time.' In the old time, too, ghosts were plentiful and, like all the island children, the little boy was afraid of them. At night, in particular, it was only when he was in bed with his parents that he felt truly safe. But even parents were not always a safeguard against a ghost.

> My mother was lying there and my father's there and I between them. They were like heaters and I feel it very warm.

> I put the [bed] clothes down like that, pushed the
> clothes till I get the air; I was smothered, did ye know,
> under the clothes.
> And when I looked, a big fire was going, good turf
> and there was a woman looking in on the bed.
> A ginger-haired woman, light ginger hair.

The woman was looking at Dónal through the window and all the while she was watching him she was combing her long hair. Dónal drew back quickly under the bedclothes. 'I was about a quarter of an hour under the clothes. I said to myself "Maybe she's away, I will come up."' When he looked again the ghost was still there. 'I think it was one of my friends [relations]. Aye. One of my aunties was ginger; she's dead.' He retreated once more to safety between his sleeping parents. After a while he peeked for a third time and saw that the woman was still looking at him. 'Ahh, if I would be bigger, did ye know, I would have a nice view on her; a nice-skinned woman and light ginger hair.' At last even his fearful curiosity could not keep him awake: 'I was young, did ye know, and I fell asleep.'

* * *

Many Tory children of that time, girls as well as boys, had to leave school early to help their parents; Dónal was no exception. When he was twelve he started to work with his father and older brothers on the land where barley, oats and potatoes were grown for the family, and turnips for the cattle. He went fishing with his father too, in one of the old small currachs (carried easily over the head by one man), that were blunt at the prow, squared off at the stern, had no seats and used paddles instead of oars. The frames for these currachs were made from green wood pliable enough to bend, brought from the mainland, there being no trees on Tory. The ribs were bound together with horse hair and, when these were secured, frame and ribs were covered with skins, sometimes sealskin or horsehide, but usually cowhide. Boiling tar was then applied and, as it dried very quickly, a currach could be 'made today, out tomorrow fishing'. Dónal was fifteen when he began fishing in earnest. His older brother

Edward, who had been a member of a crew working out of Portadoon, went to America, and Dónal took his place in the boat. He continued fishing for four years, a period that included a stint on a trawler off Howth, Co Dublin. There were nine of crew on the trawler — seven of them from Tory — and one weekend five of the Tory men, on their day off, went to the Dublin Zoological Gardens where, Dónal told me with an abashed smile, they had hoped to see a mermaid. They were sadly disappointed, so they explored the streets of Dublin and had their photograph taken in a 'picture house'.

Almost every Tory man went to Scotland at one time or another to look for work, especially when 'there was no price for the fish and the money was scarce'. The fact that Camusmore was then a stopping place for ships sailing from Sligo to Glasgow made the journey from Tory easier and many islanders went directly to Scotland without ever touching the Irish mainland. They gathered potatoes, mended roads, cut corn with scythes and hooks, did any job, however backbreaking, that would earn the much needed money for their families. Dónal's first trip to Scotland was in 1916 and he stayed for two or three years before returning to Tory to take up fishing again; fishing herrings and ballans (small wrasse) with ring-nets, *glassán* (whiting) with limpets for bait, fishing in currachs (now more like 'wee punts with oars') in Camusmore and near the high cliffs on the north side of the island.

Some time before World War II, Dónal married Kate O'Donnell, a part of his life that he never mentioned in all of our conversations. Mary McClafferty told me about her:

> Well, Katie O'Donnell, *créatúr* [literally, 'creature' — a sympathetic interjection], God rest her, was married to Dónal Beag. And she lost four children... I seen the first and I seen the last. It was cruel.
>
> And she had a sore leg after that, the *créatúr*, she hurt her leg with a spade. It was the same with all of us at that time, you wouldn't say nothing, you wouldn't go near the nurse. And the leg was always sore.
>
> No matter who will give her ointment, she would put

it on; every kind of ointment, maybe hundreds of
different kinds. And then it went septic and she got her
leg off. Aye. In Dublin. She came back and she died on
Tory soon afterwards.

Dónal had returned to Scotland for a second time in the late
1930s and, when the war started, he found work at the great
Cluny Dam — the Cluny hydro-electric system then in the
process of being constructed. It was a vast project, as Dónal
described it. 'There were *fourteen* hundred working there, and a
lot of men were killed with the blasting. There were a hundred
killed when the job was finished. Seven miles of *tunnel*. And the
tunnels were about twenty feet in height and twenty wide. For
the water for the turbines, ye know, making electric... ' Dónal
paused for a moment, remembering. 'Ah, you need to be there
yourself to know it.'

Dónal went twice to work on the dam and in the intervals
fished again on Tory. But when he came home for good after the
war, he never fished with a crew again and, as far as he knows, all
the men he used to work with in the boats are now dead. He
settled in the house just beyond and across the street from the
tower of St Colmcille. His father had left it to the family, as well
as 'as much land as would keep three houses going', some in the
west and some in the east, including bogland.

Dónal's brothers and sisters had all moved away or died
except for his sister, Peggy. She was married to Jimmy Rodgers,
but she never left the family house; and when Dónal himself
married, his wife continued to live with her family. It was the
custom with many at that time. Peggy died in 1979 and since
then Dónal has lived alone, sharing the two ground-floor rooms,
which are the only ones in use, with his battered tom-cat. The cat
is good company and Dónal has an affection for it that he will
not admit to; the cat is there, he insists, smiling, only to keep the
mice away. He has some home help, some cleaning, some
laundry and a hearty soup brought in for his evening meal, but
otherwise he takes care of himself. He eats breakfast close to
noon for, like all islanders, he goes to bed late and now that he is
old he has no need to rise early. He cooks two eggs and with

them has bread and four cups of tea, always four cups, he says firmly; much of the rest of his diet consists of milk and potatoes, which he boils in the blackened pot that hangs, as in most Tory houses, above the fire in the grate.

On the days when the weather is good and the trawler brings in the mail, he walks to the post office and visits a few friends, including Johnny Doohan. Unless the day is particularly cold and stormy, he does not kindle the turf fire in his room until after his supper; then he sits beside it, smoking a pipe while the tom-cat clings to his knee. In the last year he has had a television set but, as he is quite deaf, it is turned on in the evening as much for company as for an interest in the world outside. When not in use it is covered with a cloth. He sits alone for many hours, his thoughts unfathomable. He is a small man with a stout heart.

* * *

Visitors to Tory, particularly in the nineteenth century, always mentioned the fine physical appearance of the islanders. Mgr James Stevens wrote in his *Illustrated Handbook of South-West Donegal* (Dublin, 1872): '[Tory] has a population of 420 souls. It is inhabited by a very hardy, adventurous and stalworth [*sic*] race, the men six feet in ordinary height, and of a dark complexion; and the women noble, tall and dark-featured; and for strength and agility the Torry fishermen cannot be excelled.' William Harkin, twenty years later, also spoke of their good looks and of their independence. He continued: 'County cess or poor rate these islanders do not pay. Torry never sent a pauper to the Dunfanahy work house, nor was there a fraction of county money ever spent in making road or fence of any kind... to the present moment. Their highway is over the ocean billows, and their fences the bulwark of their fishing craft.' There are men, still, on Tory who are tall and of dark complexion, the women are good-looking and the children beautiful. No rents or rates have ever been paid in spite of the disastrous attempt by HMS *Wasp* to collect them in 1884. County money is now, however, spent on the island and it includes repairs to the one road.

Life on the island has changed considerably even in the past thirty years. For this reason I was particularly interested in hearing about the old days — of a time when all the houses were thatched; when fishing in frail currachs was the chief means of support; when the great whales and basking sharks, looking for the plentiful herring, swam within a hundred yards of the shore; and when holy water, grains of Tory's holy clay and a prayer were the fishermen's only protection. The days of Dónal's father and grandfather, when in truth 'their highway was over the ocean billows, and their fences the bulwark of their fishing craft'. I was looking forward to talking more to Dónal about what life was like on Tory when he was a small boy. I had come to know what to expect when I arrived at his house, the welcome and the conversational amenities that had to be dispensed with before settling down to taping. First of all he would comment on the weather, then, after giving me a keen look, he would announce that I was 'mending' well and follow with admonitions not to go out in the evening if it was rainy and cold (my health was excellent). After this it was my turn to say a few words, having adjusted my tone of voice to a level that seemed to work reasonably well in coping with his deafness. The session was then ready to start. On the first afternoon of taping his stories, I checked my little recorder, sat down on a chair near Dónal in front of the grate, and began by asking him if he could remember some of the things his father and mother had told him about the way of life on Tory when they were young. Having understood what I wanted he nodded.

'Is it ready?' he questioned, looking at the recorder.

'It is,' I said, 'go ahead.'

> Oh, aye. Well, I know.
> Well, he was living on fishing, fishing cods and blackjacks, going out fourteen miles on the north of the island,
> fishing with long lines.
> And putting out seaweed, seaweed for making the kelp. Selling it for two pound ten a ton. That's what he's telling me.
> And he will go out, making stacks in the harvest time,

of the seaweed; and burn it then and selling it for *two pound ten* a ton. That's cheap enough.

And then he was fishing with ring-nets,
fishing herring.

He had big family; ten of family, five boys and five girls. Reared them up with fishing and then, when the sailing boats coming from America they [the islanders] will be after them. Give them fish and 'taties' [potatoes], and they will get tea, sugar, bags of biscuits, and whiskey, wine,

and that's what my father's telling me.

And they're fishing with the long lines, cods and blackjacks. That's another kind of fish, blackfish. We call them *glasáin mhóra*, in Gaelic. *Glasáin mhóra*.

And they will salt them, cut them and clean them and after that they were selling them for three shilling a dozen. And everything was cheap here to buy — but no money.

Living in thatched houses, all thatched houses, ohhh. And they were keeping the cattle in the house, and hens in the house at that time.

My father was telling me.

The schoolhouse on Tory was built around 1865 and renovated in the 1930s. Its one large classroom was heated, in the old days, by a turf fire kept ablaze by the sod of turf that every pupil was required to bring each morning. Today the fingers and toes of the students are warmed by an electric heater, in odd contrast to the worn, brown wooden desks and to the abacus, no longer in use but still hanging on its hook on the wall. The ages of the students range, as always, from five to fourteen years, but now, after finishing the last year on Tory, some go to the mainland to continue their education at 'college' (secondary school). The school registers, at least those from 1874 to the present day, are in the Tory schoolhouse in a good state of preservation. Until the Treaty of 1921 was signed between England and Ireland, the registers were written in English. When the Treaty was ratified in 1922, and the Free State came into being, the use of Irish names, written in the beautiful Irish script, began. No longer Mary and Kathleen Duggan or Margaret Diver, Denis and Patrick Duggan or James Rodgers; but now Máire and Caitlín Ní Dhubhagáin, Maighréad Ní Dhuibhir, Donnachadh and Pádraig Ó Dubhagáin, Séamas Mac Ruairí. In the old days the children of the lighthouse keepers, of whatever denomination, attended the school as well.

In Dónal's time, perhaps because of the very large families and the great number of pupils, it seemed that, even with two schoolteachers in charge, there was a certain amount of truancy among the boys. With a smile and a chuckle Dónal told me of his infrequent attendance. Although his father, who was educated, wanted him to go to school, Dónal seldom attended the classes. 'I will rise in the morning and go to school, *yes...* I will go and hide myself all day, out after birds with snares, and my father thinking that I was in school.' But even better than snaring birds, Dónal liked sailing hand-made boats — 'wee yawls' — on Loch an Deas, the lake south-east of the lighthouse. Later I discovered that this pleasure was not limited to small truants. The lighthouse keepers showed me not only the traditional ships-in-bottles they made in their spare time, but also fine model boats, which they, too, sailed on the lake on clear days.

'Dónal,' I asked him next, 'when did you first go to sea?' I had intended to find out how old he was when he started to fish, for many boys in their early teens helped their fathers with trawl lines in the currachs or fished from the rocks; any catch meant an addition to the family income. But after only a moment of thought, Dónal answered.

> I was with my father. A drifter, a wee drifter, came out in the bay there. Fishing herring,
> a drifter, a Scotch drifter.
> And my father told me to go along in the wee currach. I was glad when I went to sea! I liked the nice ride I was getting in the currach.
> And my father had good English, and he was talking to the skipper of the wee drifter. Fishing with herring nets.

And Séamus Ward was keeping a pub that time, keeping whiskey, and wine and beer, stout; keeping a big place that time.

And when we got alongside with the drifter, he [the skipper] throw a wee cod down in the currach, and he come in himself with us,

I remember.

And he was sitting in the middle of the currach and I was sitting at the back and my father was paddling the currach with a *ceaslaí* [paddle], we call it.

And he come in below the schoolhouse, I remember that. I was a wee thing.

And I followed my father and the skipper up, and my father led him over to the pub, at Wards. And I know, I got a bottle of lemonade. *I got a bottle of lemonade.* I think a lot of that.

Ohhhh, that time!

And the skipper gave me a bottle of lemonade and he drank whiskey himself, a glass of whiskey and another glass for my father.

Two glasses of whiskey and a bottle of lemonade!

And my father saw a man passing. He was a friend to my father. 'Come on in,' he says and he gave *him* another glass. That's three glasses and a bottle of lemonade;

and I think the bottle of lemonade was good!

* * *

In the old days almost every Tory family owned sheep. As soon as the corn had been cut and the last potato stored, the animals were allowed to roam freely; during the growing season, however, they had to be watched carefully. In the west end, not far from the lighthouse, on the south side between Loch an Deas and the sea, there is a huge enclosure known as the *mainnir* (sheepfold). Its stone walls, scarcely touched by time and storms, are well over six feet in height and were built more than a hundred years ago by the sheep owners in the west end who worked together on its construction on Sunday afternoons after

Mass. The sheep were penned here during the summer nights. The east end sheep were herded on to Tor Mór, above Portadown. No walls were needed here, the cliffs were barrier enough and the approach to them so narrow that a plank or gate put across the entrance was sufficient to keep them from wandering. Dónal's older brother, when a boy, watched the sheep in the west end, 'and he was not getting but two pound ten for the six months.' When he was older he fished with a crew for a few years and then left Tory. Dónal told me with a touch of sadness, 'When he grew big, my brother, he went to America. And he went to a place called Camden in [New] Jersey. He grew up fishing, the same as my father. And he went to America. And he died in America.'

* * *

The wind can rise quickly around Tory, even in the summer. The sea becomes choppy and covered with white-caps ('white teeth' Patsy Dan Rodgers calls them), and often the wind strengthens and turns into a gale. An excellent description of what can happen is given in delightful Victorian prose by William Harkin. On a summer morning in 1892, Harkin and a group of friends boarded the 'magnificent new steamer "Melmore"' at Mulroy Bay for a special excursion to Tory and to Arranmore Island, which lies twenty miles south-east of Tory, near the coast. 'The vessel was gaily decorated with flags and bunting, and wore her holiday attire in every respect... the weather looked extremely fine.' Having enjoyed a few hours on Tory looking at the antiquities, the group returned to the ship and Captain Mitchell weighed anchor and proceeded west, taking a course towards the Arranmore lighthouse. 'It was about three p.m.' wrote Mr Harkin, 'and it just illustrates the capricious nature of the Donegal climate when we relate that the waters were showing signs of roughness quite at variance with their placid condition in the morning.' The glass was falling rapidly so it was decided to turn and head back to Mulroy, and soon they found themselves off Tory again in what had now become almost gale force winds. As the waves grew more turbulent, the captain assured the passengers of the sea-worthiness of his vessel. But although this was no doubt comforting, it did not prevent the approach of seasickness and some among the group 'experienced a most indescribable sensation adown the perpendiculars'. By now the sea was 'rolling mountains high and the foaming billows washed over the ship with angry howl. The sea-birds shrieked with fear for a perfect storm was raging.' However, after lying in Tory Sound for an hour with full steam on, they were able to steer to the mainland, and arrived safely at Mulroy House Pier (a distance of twenty-eight and a half nautical miles from Tory) 'after one of the pleasantest and most exciting seavoyages in our log book'.

The steamer *Melmore* was advertised as sailing on 'The Grand Tour to the North-West of Ireland,... specially built for this trade... fitted throughout with electric light... sailing regularly from the 13th June until the end of September, unless prevented by unforeseen circumstances'. If this 'magnificent' ship had some difficulty with a Tory storm, how was it possible for the small, frail Tory currachs to survive? Many, of course, did not. Dónal told me of the gale that was responsible for the death of his grandfather and six other fishermen.

> Well, I never saw him. But that's my mother's father, Roger, Roger Doohan you call him.
>
> And a lot of the currachs went out to the middle of the channel, fishing cods. A gale come.
>
> And did ye know that time they were going with wee currachs? Aye, paddling, and one sitting at the back.
>
> And a gale come, going sixty mile an hour to seventy mile an hour.
>
> And some of the currachs come through. My mother's uncle, he come through it, but there was two currachs missing,
>
> two currachs missing.
>
> And my grandfather was lost that day. He went to the other side of [Bloody] Foreland. And that man was along with him, they're saying he was very old. And my grandfather was young.
>
> And my mother had a sister, that's all the family at

that time when my father was lost. And she was only twelve years old, my mother; and my aunt, that's her sister, was ten years old when the father was lost.

And they were blowed out at a place called Carraig na nEascann [Rock of the Eels]. That's Gaelic. That's what you call the place.

Old Charlie was along, a man called old Charlie. A rock was submerged or something, he didn't see the rock. And the currach ran up on the rock.

And he jumped out, my grandfather, and he pushed the currach out.

And the currach went away, and old Charlie was in the currach and he wasn't able to paddle the currach to *lift* him. And he died on the rock, my grandfather.

He was a day and a half standing on the rock. And the islanders on Inishmaan and them were watching him, and they didn't go out to lift him.

And the other fellow died on the beach, after the currach went in. And they got the two dead on the beach.

And the priest who was there buried them in the cemetery there. That's what my mother was telling me about.

And the priest [who] was on the island here, he went over to see what it cost to bury them. And the priest over there, he wouldn't take no money.

'That's all right,' he says. 'I'll bury them,' he says. 'It's all right.'

And that was cruel that time. My mother herself, she was only twelve year, and the sister ten.

And they had relations in America, and they're sending the money to start them a wee shop. For the two girls and their mother.

And they were making a living in the wee shop, tea and sugar and all, things like that. Whiskey, and selling whiskey dram. And that's the way they were making a living.

* * *

Some of the fishermen could swim, but the majority could not. It was amazing that any survived when thrown into the cold waves, hampered as they were by heavy jerseys, rain gear and sometimes rubber boots. Although the Tory men seldom hesitated to come to the assistance of a drowning man and, in fact, often made heroic efforts to do so, there were those from along the mainland coast, and from the islands near by, who would not. The believed that if they rescued someone who was drowning, they themselves would sooner or later suffer the same fate; the fairies were taking them away and 'the sea must get its own'. They would not allow the body of a drowned man in the house and sometimes they would not even use timber from a boat that had been wrecked with loss of life. This is why Dónal's grandfather was left to die on the rocks off Bloody Foreland. Dónal continued his tales of storms at sea.

> They were out one time in the north, nor'west of the lighthouse, and all the boats were out.
>
> And the gale come, going ninety mile an hour, the gale.
>
> And they were making for the land when the skipper said, 'Don't be afraid,' he said, 'I will take you to the lighthouse. I'm able to manage,' he said.
>
> And every boat was doing for themselves.
>
> 'I will manage to the lighthouse, I wouldn't manage *after* that,' he said. For they have to go to Greenport to be *safe*.
>
> And another man jumped up, he put his hand on his [the skipper's] shoulder.
>
> 'Well I will take you to the Greenport,' he says, the other fellow. 'While you take us to the lighthouse,' he says, '*I* will take us to the Greenport.'
>
> A wee bit of the sail going in, a wee bit of the sail. And when they got to the lighthouse, 'Now,' says the skipper, 'where is the other man?'
>
> 'I'm the other man,' the fellow says. 'No *sail* no more,' he says, 'going with *oars*: put the four oars out!'
>
> When the big wave come — *backing*. When the wave

will go down, 'Pull away now,' he says. 'Pull away now, pull away!' When the weak wave rise again, '*Keep back*, keep back.'

When the wave will drop down again, '*Pull now* away again, away again.'

He done that till past Hill's wee house — did ye know the wee house? — and they turn up to Greenport.

In the days when all the roofs on Tory were thatched and the Tory men were, according to William Harkin, 'hardy, adventurous and stalworth', Dónal's great-grandfather made a sea voyage with a crew to Co Mayo. Perhaps no sailing ship with a captain willing to barter sugar, tea and flour for fish and potatoes had passed by the island for a long time. Whatever the reason, the island families must have been in great need, for Mayo is a long way to travel in a smack (a small fishing boat). Just before leaving Mayo, having bartered their dried fish for flour, sugar and tea, one of the smack's crew, Liam Óg (Young William), heard a girl singing as she watched a drove of cattle on 'the nice morning with the sun rising over', the morning on which the Tory men sailed home. Liam Óg memorised the song and brought it back to the island. Before singing it to me in Irish one rainy afternoon, Dónal gave me the 'meanings'.

> *My* mother was telling me about it, her grandfather was on the boat. Was on the boat. Going to a place called Mayo, in a *smack*.
>
> And they had a cargo of fish, dry fish, cods.
>
> And they went in in this port. And they made a bargain with the man in the shop, to buy [barter] the fish. And getting food *back*. Bags of meal, bags of flour and tea and sugar.
>
> And when they made a bargain about that, they have to get a place to stay for the night. Ye know. And there's no place.
>
> They're wild people over there that time, did ye know, and everybody there was strange to *them*, to Tory.

> And there was a man dead there; there was a *wake* there.
>
> And when they hauled up the boat and everything, and they hauled the provisions down with a cart, down ready for the morning, they went in the place the wake was on.
>
> And the Tory men, four of them, come in. And as the other people were coming in, they will go above where the body was laying.
>
> Well, I will say, this is the bed now; and old women and all, and young men and old men came in and cry above the body.

Dónal got up from his chair by the fire and went to the bench against the wall upon which his old grey and white cat was sleeping, having been dislodged on my arrival from its perch on the old man's knee. Throwing his cap on the floor, then crossing himself, Dónal cupped his hands behind his ears and gave a long ululating cry.

> That's the crying they have. You know the way. I'm not able to do it right, did ye know; it was like a bagpipe. Crying like that, and they have to do it three times on the body that was dead.
>
> And the Tory men walk in: they didn't know nothing about the things here.
>
> And, 'It's a funny thing, you're strange,' he [the man of the house] says, 'coming in here, getting plenty smoke and taking plenty to eat, and you wouldn't cry on the body.'
>
> He say something about *feannadh an phocáin* [literally 'skinning the goat' — a wake game]. 'You should do it,' he says. Here they didn't *know* what he was saying. *Feannadh an Phocáin.* I don't know about that word. That's in Gaelic. It's a different Gaelic.
>
> And, 'You should do that,' he says.
>
> They were sitting there all night and people coming

crying about [Dónal cried again]. And the Tory men there. No word about that.

And then they went down [to the harbour], when the day was coming on; and a *nice* morning, and the sun was rising over.

That's in County Mayo. They were going any place that time.

And when the sun was going up, a nice woman was coming over, a young girl, watching a drove of cattle.

And she had a nice song. A nice song in the morning.

And one of the men that was on the boat, he was listening. 'Dear, oh dear, that's a nice song she sung,'

in Gaelic, a Gaelic song.

He ran up to her. And she stand. And the drove of the cattle was about a dozen, going on.

They call that *an eadra*; before they milk them in the morning they have to go out and get some of the grass, did ye know, and they put them in again and milk them.

And, 'Will ye sing the song again?' he says.

'Oh, did ye like the song?'

'Yes,' he says, 'I like the song.'

And she sang it again, singing the song,

and he was listening. He was listening.

And he gave her two shillings and he tapped her arm, like that. 'It's a nice song, I have it now,' he says; and he was going on the boat, the cargo was in. 'I have it now.'

The man they call Liam Óg. That's the man that brought the song to the island.

* * *

In 1984, Fr Dermot Ó Péicín, the island priest at the time, showed me an original copy in his possession of the early morning edition of *The Times* of London, dated September 24, 1884. He kindly gave me a photocopy of the pertinent page. In two long columns, with reports from Dublin and Cork, the shocking news was told of the sinking of HMS *Wasp* off the Tory lighthouse with the loss of fifty men, including all officers. Six men were rescued from the rocks: the cook, the quartermaster, two marines, and two seamen.

Robin Fox explained the reason behind the voyage of Her Majesty's frigate to Tory. '[The islanders] refused to pay rates as well as rents. The "collector of county cess" was driven off the island in 1871 and, at Lifford Assizes, it was decided that the armed forces should be used to collect the arrears (£263 15s 8d). This was easier to order than to carry out and it was not until 1884... that the expedition was mounted.' The reason for the wreck of the *Wasp* was eventually attributed by the British Admiralty to 'navigational error' but, even in the first accounts in *The Times*, there seem to me to be occasional discrepancies. 'Of one thing all who know her brave and popular commander are convinced, that there was no cessation of vigilance or care on his part, as he was unremitting in his attention to duty, and conscious of the danger of the coast, would not leave the deck for an instant.' A report later that same night stated, however, that as the boat was nearing Tory, 'after passing Arranmore Island... Lieutenant Nicholson [the commanding officer] gave the course to the man at the wheel and turned into his cabin. Some hours after, the man at the wheel told the chief of the watch that he feared they were not keeping clear enough of the island, as he could see the lighthouse, and the vessel, with the short sail, was drifting to leeward. This was communicated to the captain whose reply was that the man must steer the course that was directed by his superior officer, and that all would be right. There are some conflicting accounts of what followed... '

Having heard so much about the *Wasp*, and having read the report in *The Times*, I was curious to hear an islander's version of what had happened. I asked Dónal to tell me the story; it was one he must have told often and he was delighted to have the opportunity to do so again.

> Well. The PK was here at the time, PK, keeper in charge [of the lighthouse]. Stocker you call him. And there was a helping man.
> That's the beginning of the story.
> There was a helping man there called Billy Duggan, I

was talking to Billy. And Billy was a young man, that time, he wasn't twenty, a strong big man, strong man.

And the two of them were up at the top of the lighthouse.

And Stocker say with Billy, 'Did ye hear the gulls screaming?' he says. 'They're going very late *tonight*, the *gulls*.'

Billy says, 'No gulls. That's the screamings of men there,' he say.

'Ah you're wrong,' Stocker says, 'that's gulls,' he says.

'No,' Billy says — Billy was telling *me* — 'that's the screamings of men.'

'Did ye think? Well make ready the lamp,' Stocker says. 'Make ready the lamp till we go down, till we see.'

And Billy made ready the lamp.

And when Billy was going down and putting the lamp up at the wall, to jump down from the wall, the survivors put their hands *in*.

And they had *bed* clothes on them, the bed sleeping clothes on them. And, *five* of them have come over, put their hands in, over the wall.

There was a long pause, so long that, thinking to refresh his memory, I asked Dónal if there had been a high wind blowing on the evening of the wreck. I should have realised that I was interrupting the story as he always told it. He waited politely until I had finished and then continued.

When Stocker put up his hand to jump down with the lamp, the survivors put their hands *in*.

That's the *beginning* of story, *you know now*. [Dónal spoke reprovingly.]

And then, Stocker turned up to the lighthouse again with the survivors. Take them up and heat them up and put dry clothes on them.

And how many escaped? One, two, three, four, *five*. There should be *six*. But there's one that's not up at the lighthouse. There's *five* and one missing.

'Make ready the lamp again,' Billy says, 'till we go down and get the other man that's missing.'

And they were searching around the place, and they had seen him sitting beside a rock.

And, 'This is you? You're living?'

'Yes, I'm here. I'm here.'

'And *what* way you come?'

'Ah, I didn't come at all. A wave come in and leave me beside the rock. A wave at sea, come in.

'I was waiting for another wave to take me out again, and I didn't get no wave, I'm sitting here, simple.'

He was the cook and he'd been making ready food, and he was closing up to sixty year old.

And Billy made ready and he carried him up on his back. And Stocker was holding the lamp. Billy was a strong man, a strong *young* man that time, twenty.

And he carry him and leave him up at the lighthouse. The same as the rest. That's six was saved. And that's the beginning of the story about the *Wasp*.

And she left County Mayo in the morning, before the lights appeared,

in the dark.

And they were in the bar, the crew of the man-o-war, the *Wasp*. Fifty-two her crew, and one of them was drunk, and he wasn't able to stand, and he had to lie [stay] back, he wasn't able to go aboard,

he had too much whiskey.

And they were making for Tory Island, to evict them off from the island, and it was blowing tremendously, ninety mile an hour, form the northern.

And *three* sails. *Three* sails.

The *Wasp* was built of timber. *Teak wood.* Bars of brass going through the skin and inside the ribs. And screws up. And a one gun. And a wee engine. And *three sails.* And fifty-two her *crew.*

And she run in between two rocks — I know the rocks, I was fishing there — and one of the rocks, five foot above the water and the other rock *submerged. Can't see.*

And when then, when she run in, Captain Nicholls was the captain, the commander. And the quartermaster was at the wheelhouse. And Captain Nicholls went out of his mind,

he lost his mind.

And all the crew on the south side of the *Wasp* was waiting for the commander's *order*. They're not supposed to jump on the rock till they got the word of the *commander.*

And no, the commander went out of his mind. And those survivors jumped on their own without orders. And if the commander will give them orders they'd be *all safe.*

They jump, and a big wave come in.

A big wave of sea come in, and the *Wasp* she rise up like that, up, up, up, up like that and then she was dragged on the deep and she capsized, did ye know.

She capsized and *all* the crew lost their lives beneath the ship.

According to *The Times,*
The *Wasp*, they say, had been 30 hours under sail from Westport, it not being considered necessary to employ steam, as there was plenty of time to reach Moville... Information has been received in Londonderry that on the night before the wreck of the *Wasp* two fishermen who went out in a boat to look after their lobster pots were drowned within 200 yards of the shore on the same coast, their boat having been upset in a storm. . . [At a meeting of the Fishery, Piers and Harbour Commission] a resolution was passed expressing deep regret [at the loss] and bearing testimony to the care, skill, and efficiency with which the vessel was navigated by Commander Nicholls...

After telling me about the sinking of the *Wasp*, and about Billy Duggan, who had helped rescue the few survivors, Dónal said that he would 'think on' the ballad of the *Wasp* that night when he went to bed and would sing it for me the next day. He always kept his promises and so was waiting eagerly when I walked into his house the following afternoon. As he sang, with his usual enthusiasm, I thought of Patsy Dan's comment that if Dónal couldn't remember the words, he made them up as he went along.

Well listen now. It's the beginning of the song:

It's on the twenty-second of September on the year of '84,
It was a boat, a steamship, called the Wasp *was her name.*
She left Westport that morning at the County of Mayo,
To visit Tory Island, and she came so far and near,
And she struck the rock on Tory
And she never rise no more.

Oh, it was a dreadful sight that morning
Before the lights appear,
And the wind was blowing tremendously
Around the northern shore.
Six of her survivors was washed off ashore,
And while fifty-two of her noble crew
Were sink in the swelling sea,
Sinkin in th' Atlantic waves and never to appear no more.

Oh, Captain Nicholls was a sober man,
He will work with art and skill.
He will bring the Wasp *to every place*
And she could reach Moville.
It was eviction his duty
For the Wasp *was forced to go,*
She leave Westport that morning at the County of Mayo.

Oh, may God rest their soul, my gallant men,
They was most of them Irish men.
God look on their soul, God will be with their soul,
Now they are rest in peace. Amen.

Dónal always spoke the last line of a song, an old tradition.

His sentiment that if the crew was gallant they must, of necessity, be Irish was of course a wonderful exaggeration. Most of the *Wasp*'s crew came from around Chatham Dock in England.

Later *The Times* reported from Cork:

> A telegram received from the chief boatmen of Coastguards at Sheephaven [Co Donegal] states that Lord Leitrim sent his steam yacht Norseman to Tory Island, but the men saved from the Wasp refused to leave until an official order arrived. [Her Majesty's ship] Valiant passed Dunfanaghy at 5.30 on her way to Tory Island.

Still later:

> The Admiralty yesterday afternoon received a telegram from the captain of the Valiant, who had arrived in the vicinity of Tory Island, reporting that the sea was so very rough that nothing could be got on to the island. No boat could live in the sea then running.

The *Valiant* had to wait until the sea moderated. Meanwhile, the bodies of the drowned sailors were beginning to come ashore. Dónal continued.

> Well, listen.
>
> When the *Wasp* was lost, the bodies were coming in with the tide, on [after] the nine days they rose again. And a lot of currachs, wee currachs, was out fishing.
>
> And the priest came to my father.
>
> 'I'll give you a good sense [information, advice] now,' he says, 'to bring the dead bodies in. And beach them. And anyone you beach I will put it in the book and you can get two pound for each man.'
>
> That's the British order, did ye know.
>
> 'And you put a coffin on them, a coffin, and *bury* them yourself,
>
>   you'll get five pound.'
>
> And my father run up to my mother and my grandmother — the grandfather was lost, did you know, I was telling you that.

And my grandmother tell him, 'If you touch them,' she says, 'if *you* touch them bodies,' she says, 'you won't come in this house,'
fear of the *ghost*.
They were feared of a ghost that time, did ye *know*. She was feared that the house would be full of ghosts that night. Ohhh, he went down again and take the currach up.
The other currachs went out, and beach the bodies up. But he was getting the *first* sense, my father.
And he was sorry again after that, that he didn't do it. He will do it only for the fear about the ghost, did ye *know*. Heh, heh, heh, heh!

* * *

Pádraig Óg Rodgers told me that Tory was sometimes referred to as Oileán Cholmcille (Colmcille's Island), for the islanders regard the saint as their own. After the toss of his bishop's crosier from the top of Cnoc na Naomh — some say it was Muckish Mountain — had won Colmcille the right to build a monastic settlement on Tory, he lost little time in making the journey by currach to the island. But landing on the island was not easy. On his first attempt he was quickly driven away by the pagan inhabitants; the second attempt was equally unsuccessful. On the third try, however, as the islanders tell it (three is a significant number on Tory), he managed to step ashore from his currach onto a large rock. Here he was met, according to Manus O'Donnell, by Oillil, son of Boadan, who was 'the lord to whom the island belonged at that time... [and] not disposed to permit Colmcille to bless or abide in it'. In spite of his hostile attitude, the saint asked the lord if he would give him 'the breadth of his mantle of the island', and the request was granted for, said Oillil, 'It is no worry to me to give you that.' As soon as Colmcille spread his cloak on the rock, it expanded until it covered the whole island and the understandably outraged pagan set his venomous hound, *cú nimhe*, against the intruder. Colmcille quickly made the sign of the cross and halted the hound in its tracks where it died instantly; at which, completely overwhelmed by such Christian miracles, Oillil 'fell upon his knees, and believed in God and Colmcille and gave him the whole island'.

Some question Manus O'Donnell's story and maintain that it was another man, an islander, who became the first convert. John O'Donovan writes:

> The story related by Manus O'Donnell about Alidus, the son of Baedan, setting the dog on Colmcille on his first landing is yet remembered, and the impression of the dog's foot yet pointed out in stone. It is now stated that it was a man of the name of O'Dugan that gave the island to Colmcille. A man of that name is now the senior on that island.

TH Mason in his book *The Islands of Ireland* (London, 1936) agrees.

> The first man to take his stand beside [the saint] was a dark-featured man, and to him the saint gave the new name of Dhugan [the scarce dark man]... The saint exercised his miraculous power by banishing the rats, and conferred the same power on his first convert.

'Well listen,' Dónal said to me, 'listen.'

There were bad people on this island at that time, oh, thousands of years ago. *Pagans, all pagans*, was on the island.

And they didn't like anybody to land; only themselves. They were over at Dún, Tor Mór, living there. They had a house there. And the trenches are there yet, you will see the trenches.

Aye, that was Balor's; a man called Balor, a bad man. He was a pirate. He had a boat here and he stayed on the island.

And when the British sailing ships came over from America, they had bars of gold. And he will go out and rob them. And put the bars of gold in his boat. And take it into the island here and bury it here, at Dún.

And then he will go over the island and take milk away, and butter. And he take heifers away and kill them and eat them. And bullocks, take *them* away over and kill them and eat them.

He never give *no money* to the poor people. He will do what he likes to do, without asking,

And that was going a *long* time.

And if any people will try to come in, he will be down on the rocks chasing them away.

And Colmcille come out in a currach one day — you'll see him rowing in the chapel. You'll see him in the [stained glass] window.

Ah, he couldn't get to come in, Colmcille. He couldn't get an inch on the rock; they chased him away. Colmcille went away.

'Well,' he says, 'when I will come again,' he says, 'I will *land*. No matter there's about *badness*, I will land.'

And when he come the third time, he had the *brat* [mantle], you call it. Colmcille landed like that.

'I'm only wanting a foot square,' he says [to the pagan], 'on the rock.'

This man [Duggan] come to him. 'You get back,' Colmcille says, 'keep at the *back* of me,' he says. He's going to do it [stay] *that* time.

The good people was very scarce, and that's the way Colmcille made the name Duggan; that's the day he gave the name. *Dubh-gann*, 'black-scarce', you put it, 'black scarce'.

* * *

I knew about the large rock partly covered by the yellow lichen that is at the edge of the sea below Gracie and John Joe McClafferty's house. I had seen the four clear indentations, the paw marks made by the poison hound when, at the pagan lord's command, it leapt to attack Colmcille; and the narrow cleft in the rock behind, cut by the hound's tail as it propelled itself towards its intended victim. I'm afraid I interrupted Dónal again to ask him about *cú nimhe*, a dog that, it is said, may have been a rabid greyhound. He gave me a reproachful look. 'I'm telling you, I didn't get as far as *that*, did ye know.' I apologised and he continued.

> Oh, aye, they had the hound for *badness*. If the hound would look at you like that — you're *dead*.
>
> Aye, they had the bad hound and everything. That's the reason Colmcille came in and chased them *away*. After that it was a holy island. And he build a tower down there, for keeping the bad people from coming in.
>
> And *I* seen one time there was a graveyard. All where you see the sea coming in, that at *that* time, was all grass growing. And there was a *cemetery*, from the tower to the other wee graveyard.
>
> And all the people was buried there, on the island.
>
> Aye, they were taking them in here from the mainland, and burying them here, in the holy place.

William Rodgers told me that bodies were brought from as far away as Co Mayo for burial on Tory. Men carried them, he said, in a *ciseán* (basket) made of straw, with straw handles. If the weather was stormy when they reached Magheraroarty, they would bury the bodies in the great sand dunes and wait for a good day to take them in. If the storm lasted too long, they left them in the dunes. James Coll of Magheraroarty told William, 'We give eye to that place one time to set spuds in it, on account of the sand. The *first thing* we got was bodies. Heads. Bones.' When the winter gales would wash away some of the ground from the old Tory graveyard near the sea, Dónal, as a young boy, saw the skeletons of those who had been buried there long ago, lying between stone flags. Among the bones lay brass medals. 'The string was away,' Dónal told me, 'only the medal is lying there.' They were about six inches in length, heavy, and shaped like a triangle, or, as William Rodgers described them, 'like a church door'.

Said Dónal, 'All Latin was written on them. You can't find out the names.'

* * *

'And many's a time my mother was cursing on that man, Hughie Diver you call his name.' So Dónal ended a story, told to me earlier, about his mother and the cat that turned into a man. He spoke so often of someone 'cursing on' another person that I asked Patsy Dan Rodgers about it. 'Were they just speaking angrily or were they really cursing?'

'Oh,' replied Patsy, 'they were cursing, no doubt about it, and very angrily indeed.' He then told me of the afternoon when, as a small boy, he walked into a neighbour's kitchen and saw the old woman sitting in a chair by the hearth. To his amazement, as he watched, she pulled her skirt above her knees, rolled down her stockings and 'went down on her knees like a gannet diving for mackerel — and she had the knees for it.' And the tears streamed down her cheeks for she wished such bad luck to come upon the one she was cursing that she would be forced to weep.

TH Mason wrote:

> The *clocha breaca* (speckled stones) [on Inishmurray Island, Co Sligo] are the celebrated cursing stones, some of which are ornamented. They are placed on top of a rude erection of uncut slabs of rock. When a person desires to call down a malediction on one who had wronged him, he turns the stones contrary to the way of the sun — ie right to left... woe betide the party, however, who seeks the aid of the stones undeservedly or wrongly as, in such case, the curse falls on the head of him who has worked it.

Mason mentioned pilgrimages but did not say if they were rituals connected with the use of the *clocha breaca*. If they were not, the mere act of turning the stones anti-clockwise seems simple enough. On Tory, turning the cursing stone was a far more arduous undertaking and, as on Inishmurray, woe betide the one who used the cursing stone wrongly. For Tory there was an added danger: whenever the stone was turned successfully, Patsy Dan said, 'Seven years of bad luck would come upon the community; the island; so to say, hunger — if it was worked properly.'

'Why did they use the stone then?' I asked him, wondering if such a disaster was worth the cursing.

'For their own advantage. I mean their own advantage, in those days, was too important to them. They were poor and they hadn't much, so they couldn't be any worse off.'

The stone could be used for both good and evil. Patsy Dan told me, 'When you walk against the sun, that's the *turas* [journey] for the cursing; and when you give your back to the sun, kind of *go* with the sun, then that's for saving souls.' When I asked Dónal about the *turas* and the turning of the stone, he gave me his usual detailed, and dramatic version.

> Well, listen. Listen now.
>
> There was a man, a *holy* man, what you call Colmcille.
>
> That's the man who owned the stone, and that's the man who made the stone, to keep your enemies from coming *in*. And you use the stone the same way. And before you turn the stone, you have to make the *turas* around the island, and you have to go in your bare feet, did ye *know*.
>
> And in the morning before, you have to start before the sun rises. And you have your beads, praying. Praying to God. And Colmcille.
>
> Around, going *east*.
>
> And there was a flat stone, blue, the mark of a foot on it, down below the wall.
>
> And you have to stand, before you start, on this flat stone.
>
> And you stand like that: no *socks*. *No boots*. Feet bare.
>
> And then you have your beads and pray, gong east.
>
> Going out in every rough place. Stones, rough, to get your feet cut.
>
> *Bloodness*.
>
> Round and round; around over by the lighthouse on the north, and away down by the lighthouse and coming around to another stone where you put a tolly [a tally].
>
> And you can't speak with no one. If you meet man or woman, you can't speak.
>
> Tomorrow do the same.

> Nine mornings. You can't turn the stone till the nine mornings will be finished.
> And then when the nine mornings are finished you go to the stone. And turn the stone.
> That's Colmcille's stone.

Dónal got up from his chair and went to the table under the window upon which he keeps a small round mirror on a stand, a comb, and a china plate holding a piece of soap. Taking the plate and the soap he returned to his chair and, sitting down again, he put them on the floor in front of him. Leaning forward, he began to manipulate them. There was, he explained, a 'flag' at the bottom, six feet long; then a flat stone, the 'right one'. On top; in between, a 'marble stone, like an egg'. For the demonstration, the floor was the flag, or big stone, the 'right one' was the plate, and the piece of soap was the egg-shaped 'marble'. He continued his story as he moved the pieces about. Having read of the *clocha breaca*, a 'marbled' stone seemed within the realm of possibility.

> The nine mornings is finished making the *turas*. You have to be up early and you have to start before the sun rises. And listen now. You have to have your prayer for turning the stone. And that's the way.
> There's a round stone like that [he picked up the soap] and a flat stone like that [lifting the plate]. And then you're going to turn the stone. It's ready to turn. People think to turn it *that way*. [Dónal rotated the plate.]
> No. That's wrong. You *lift* it like that. Now, wait till you see. [He turned the plate over.] Touch here the bottom one. And say your prayer and your beads. Colmcille prayed, for turning the stone. Ready now to turn. Wait till I tell you.
> You have to turn three times. That's the first time. [He turned the plate over and, at the same time, slipped the piece of soap under it.]
> Say your prayer now.

> And *then*, you're ready again; say your prayer again, for you're going to lift it again.
>
> That's the second time. You're going to turn it on your enemies, did ye know.
>
> This is the third time. Turn now. [For the third time, he slipped the 'egg' under the 'stone'.]

'I always thought that the stone was really turned. And now I see that it was not turned at all, it was lifted,' I exclaimed.

Dónal was delighted. 'No turn! No turn! Heh, heh. No turn at all, ye know. Heh, heh, heh. People don't know the history. I knew the man who had the book and the history and all and was telling me about it. Aye. That's the way you turn the stone.'

* * *

It is said that the six sons and the beautiful daughter of the king of India came to Tory in search of Colmcille and expired from the weariness and strain of their long journey. They are known as the *mórsheisear* (big six, ie seven). Lifted from their boat, they were brought to life by Colmcille, whereupon, having been given absolution, according to Manus O'Donnell, 'they died again forthwith... [Colmcille] ordered a solemn burial and the erection of a little temple over them. The temple of the seven is its name from that day to this — *Mor-seisear*'. When, as all the stories tell, the woman was found on top of the grave for three mornings in a row, Colmcille, O'Donnell continues, 'blessed and consecrated a spot for herself apart, outside the temple, to the west thereof, a little short distance from it, and she was buried there and her corpse did not rise out of the ground from that time forward. And great was the number of portents and miracles that were effected from the clay in which she was buried, from that time, till now.' And still the eldest of the Duggans collects the clay from a place near the ruins of the little chapel, known to this day as Teampall an Mhórsheisir (Temple of the Seven).

I knew that the Tory fishermen always carried some of the holy clay with them, either in a pocket or tucked away in the bow of the boat. They were frightened, and with good reason, of the whales and basking sharks that hunted the many shoals of herring that swam near the shore in those days. As Patsy Dan told me, 'They could hardly go a number of hundreds of yards away until they would meet with one of those sea animals at all times.'

'Jimmy Duggan gave me some of the holy clay a year ago,' I told Dónal. 'I hope it will work as well in a car or in an airplane as in a currach!'

Dónal assured me that it was good for all kinds of travel, or anything that meant to harm me. 'You carried it, of course, when you went fishing,' I asked, 'for good luck? To keep you safe?'

> Aye. For safe. We take it in our pocket in a wee piece of *cloth*.
>
> And we have fear of the big whales, you know. The whales, big, ohhhh, *big* animals. Like a row of houses. Big as that.
>
> And basking sharks. Bad.
>
> Well, we are taking the holy soil, the holy clay, in a wee pocket of cloth. When we see the shark going in the water, and there will be danger — some will be jumping out of the water — we put the holy clay out,
>
> and we wouldn't see them no more.
>
> If the whale will run after you, you put the holy soil out. And she wouldn't go farther than *that*, the whale. *Finish*.
>
> And that's what the holy clay is for, to keep the badness away from you that's carrying the soil.

'It must have been very frightening to be out in a boat, especially a small currach, when there were whales around,' I said.

> Oh, aye. They would follow you sometimes, and you didn't know what they were going to do, did ye know.
>
> Now I seen a boat. And she ring a *ráth* [shoal] of herring.

They caught the herring and they were filling the boat, putting their cargo in from the net.

And a whale rise like that; she was hunting; she heed the smell of the herring. And she run above the boat and she went down and she break the boat in two halves. I seen that.

And the boat was near the land, and the crew was safe. They lost all the herring. I seen that myself. Aye.

Did you ever see a whale? Eh? Well. A whale now. From William Rodgers' house down there to where Paddy O'Donnell is — that length.

And one swallowed a boat. Oh, she swallowed a boat over at Teelin a few years ago. A big whale.

And they was out fishing cods and a big whale come in and she rise like that, and she swallow the eight men was in the boat. A skiff of a boat. No word about them no more.

It was about sixty years ago. My father was talking to a man — he was fishing over at Teelin, this happened at Teelin over there, and my father was talking to the man who was out fishing the day that the whale swallowed the boat. Aye.

And the man was forward rowing the boat, forward when the whale jumped. Closed her mouth, he says and away down, the skiff and eight of crew.

A year after Dónal told me this story, I had the good fortune to talk to Seán Ó hEochaidh, who comes from Teelin, and who, before beginning forty years of collecting material for the Folklore Department at University College, Dublin, was a fisherman himself. This is the way he heard it:

Well, in the first instance, I'm surprised that they had the version of this story on Tory Island, the story of the man who was devoured by the *whale*. Really that was a South Donegal story. And I actually *worked* with the *son* of the man who was devoured by the whale.

It happened in Inver. Inver is a little fishing village in

South Donegal; half way, I'd say, between Donegal town and Killybegs. And in the old days, the little Inver Bay there was a great place for both herring and sprat. Especially the sprat came there in shoals, during the summer months; especially during the summer month of May — and June. When the weather was good, in fact when the weather was hot. Not like we're having at the present time.

Well anyhow. They fished these sprat, and of course in small boats; and instead of using nets — they had not nets *suitable* at that time to catch these — they used an outfit which they called a loop; and that was a long pole, and the handle of this thing was about twenty feet long, with a net on the end of it, a circular net like the landing net which is used at the moment by anglers to net salmon or trout.

Now in those days as well, so long ago, it was very rarely that men wore boots at all. Because up until *my* own time I saw men going around in their bare feet, I saw men mowing hay and working in the bog, cutting turf, in their bare feet. But, when fishing, they sometimes wore socks; they never knew of course what wellingtons, or rubber boots, were at the time, or for years afterwards.

And that man that I worked with was this man's son, who was Tommy Raughter, and he told me the story about the sort of death that his father had. He told me that story about these men being out in this small boat fishing for these sprat. Now, I might mention that the sprat is a small fish about the size of a sardine, or maybe a little larger than the sardine.

But *he* was looping the sardine and they were there by the million. And he was doing very well and lo-and-behold this monster, sea monster, got up at the bow of the boat and opened its jaws and devoured the whole bow of the boat that he was fishing on. Now the last thing that the man in the stern, as I was telling you, saw was this man's dyed socks — he wore a pair of socks which was dyed by lichen, which was scraped off the stones at that time and used as a dye locally, a lovely brown colour — and that was the last that he saw of his pal, the socks going down the monster's throat. And that was the end of him.

'I've been coming to Tory for several years,' I said to Dónal, 'and I've never seen a sign of a whale. I've seen a seal, but not a whale. What has happened to them?' Dónal explained 'When I was at school, you wouldn't see the sea at all with whales. And basking sharks. They're killing them now and taking oil out of them. And they're getting scarce now for *that*!' I know that it will never happen now, that when I walk the road to Portadoon and look south, or sit in a sheltered spot in the northern cliffs, I will only see the commercial trawlers ploughing heavily through the grey seas. But at least I can imagine that one day as I look towards the horizon, my eyes may suddenly glimpse, for even a brief moment, a vast dark object in the water moving slowly and majestically: a monstrous and prodigious whale, a whale the length of the distance from William Rodgers' house to the house of Paddy O'Donnell.

Sir William Wilde (1815–1876), one of the first collectors of Irish folklore, wrote in *Irish Popular Superstitions* (Dublin, 1852):

> The fairies, the whole pantheon of Irish demigods are retiring, one by one, from the habitations of man to the distant islands where the wild waves of the Atlantic raise their foaming crests... or they have fled to the mountain passes and here have taken up their abodes in those wild romantic glens — lurking in the gorgeous yellow furze and purple heath, amidst the savage disrupted rocks...

I have not spent much time in the wild romantic glens but I know well the coast of Tory where wild waves of the Atlantic raise their foaming crests all too often. Since I have started collecting stories, the thoughts of the fairies that must surely have 'retired' to this distant island was often foremost in my mind.

When I returned to Tory in the spring of 1985, Dónal had just recently moved back into his house after spending, for the first

time, the winter months with a niece in Falcarragh. He looked a
little pale and he seemed to move more slowly. When he is on his
own, he putters around doing small chores: boiling potatoes,
bending down to put milk in the cat's dish, making tea, laying
the fire, visiting friends when the weather is reasonable, and
going to the post office. I suspected that his niece had looked
after him so well that there was little or nothing for him to do
but sit in a comfortable armchair. Falcarragh is a small quiet
coast town, not far from Magheraroarty where the Tory boats
land when they go to the mainland. There is one unobtrusive
factory near by that manufactures knitwear. From one of the
curves of Ballina Road, where some of the Tory families now live
in council houses, one can see the island nine miles away. At
times, it stands out so clearly that it looks as though it was
anchored only a short distance from the shore. The winds blow
fresh from the North Atlantic. Dónal was scornful, however. 'The
air was so foul,' he told me, 'I was gasping for breath like a crow.'
He was glad to be back on Tory in his own house with his cat,
and in several weeks he was his old self again.

The cat was pleased to see him but it was becoming
increasingly jealous of me. It was usually sitting on Dónal's lap
when I came into the room. As the old man moved slightly to
greet me and push the cat from his knee, it would try to avoid
the inevitable journey to the floor by digging its claws into
Dónal's trousers and braking hard, a manoeuvre that never
succeeded. Once on the linoleum, it would sit and glare at me,
the markings on its face already giving it a permanent frown. A
few wipes of its paw over its ears and nose to restore its self-
possession, and it would get up, walk stiffly to the bench against
the wall, jump on to it and curl up. It always lay with its back to
me, a final expression of hostility.

When I went to see Dónal the evening after my arrival, the
clouds were low, dark grey and heavy with rain. The weather, I
gathered, had not been good for quite a while and I thought of
Dónal's remark the year before, after an equally long spell of
dismal days, 'I think the sun needs new batteries!' As I walked
along in my old green raincoat with the hood, avoiding puddles
and wondering when the next shower would come, it occurred

to me that this was an appropriate time to ask Dónal about ghosts and fairies. And so, having drawn up my chair to the fire, and watched the cat perform its usual ritual, I told Dónal a bit of news about my family, and then suggested my topic for conversation. He agreed and began as always: 'Well. Listen. Listen.'

> This one was true, true, true. I heard. My mother was telling me about it.
>
> And her uncle wasn't married at all and none of the uncles was married. She had three uncles and they went to America. And this one came back over, just one of them.
>
> And he was stopping here on his own. And he was working away on the fields, by himself.
>
> And he was working putting out seaweed, for manuring 'taties' [potatoes], and doing everything on his own. And nobody was in the house and he wasn't married *at all.*
>
> And one night he come over *late* and he had no turf *in.* No turf.
>
> And he took an empty bag with his hand, like that. Oh, that's what my mother was telling *me.* An empty bag for a few sods. To make the *fire.*
>
> And he's going to make tea. He can't make bread or nothing but he's buying biscuits at the shop, to put the dinner over. And that's the way he was carrying on.
>
> And his own stack [of turf] was *there,* and there was a path going out to the stack. And it's deep at that side and deep at *that* side, and he was afraid to fall. And get *wet.*
>
> He went to another man's stack that's on the *dry.* He went out and catched the bag, like that, and put the sods in.
>
> And at the *back* of the stack he heard the *noise.* He heard the screamings, did ye know, of the people who [now dead] *owned* the stack.
>
> And then he catched the bag like that, and he had six

sods in the bag, and he's making for home. He was feared, when he heard the noise. And he run and he threw the bag away.

And the stack was in *flames*, going up. Blue flames. *Blue*.

And when he was going across the wall of the yard, going across, *three* follow him. And he knew the people and they were dead, long ago.

And the three went up on his *back*, and knock him *down*, and he was a strong man himself. The three was above him, trying to *choke* him, and *kill* him.

And he rise. He was a fine man himself, did ye know, and he rise again. And they was jumping on his back and tearing his jacket.

And he made for my mother; he was my mother's uncle. *I* seen him. And many's the time he was standing there, and he was cursing on them, on them people. They were very bad.

And it was funny the way they come.

Well. When it was over he was staggering when he's going in to my mother, staggering, staggering, staggering. Ohhhh, I heard my mother saying.

And he say to my mother, he say, 'Is my vest torn?' he say.

'Oh, there's nothing wrong with your vest — only the *noise* you're making.'

They're only *shadows* [fairies] at the time, did ye know, the three.

'Your vest is all right,' she says. But *he* heard the tear.

And there was big bowls that time. I seen them. And he drink *three* of them, of water, I heard my mother saying.

And he fill it up. And fill it again. And fill it again the three times.

And [in the end] he had no turf.

That was a true thing. Many's a time he was cursing on the people, there. Sitting there. I *seen* him.

* * *

Lights like candle flames, usually golden or blue, are considered an omen of death, although sometimes they may appear after a death has occurred. This sign is still seen on Tory. When I arrived on the island in 1985, three island men had died during the year; one of them was Willy Diver. Patsy Dan told me: 'Well Jimmy Dooley now, they buried his brother Wully about nine weeks ago; and he [Jimmy] said that he went up to make a bed upstairs, himself and the father, and that his poor brother was over on the West Village — that was about a week or two before he died — and that he saw a light — and his father saw the same light and he saw the same light the following night. And, "Jimmy," he said, "I saw a lovely light," he said, "and it went right out to the side of the window," he said. And it was a kind of bluish bright light, so to say. He could see it very, very clear indeed. And, "Well," Jimmy says, "I saw the same light." So Jimmy then had an outlook for his father, because he is well over eighty coming up to ninety, and he thought that if anything at all was going to happen that it would be his father. Instead — the light mightn't have anything to do with poor Wully either — but it was Wully they found dead on the West Village.' Dónal saw red lights the night after his sister died:

> When my sister died, there was a wake here.
>
> And she was laying in the coffin there, and I went to fetch a candle to her. My sister was very good to me, and I was good to her, the same.
>
> And the nurse came to me, Nurse Rooney was here. 'You'd better,' she says — I was up two nights — 'you'd better go to bed.'
>
> I went and I take my coat off and ready for the bed; I closed the door. And when I looked at the sideboard, there was a light on the sideboard. A light.
>
> It's not a candle, only a red light about that height. I was looking. That's wonder.
>
> And the wake was going on.
>
> The light was steady and I was looking out like that. And the light rise about a foot on the sideboard. No candle, only the light, A *red* light, And I was wonder.

> That was true now, I'm telling you, I seen it myself.
> There was hangers [shades] on the window. And the way it was, the light was coming under the gable, like that. I will lose it, I will get it again, I will lose it, I will get it again. That's the way it was *showing*.
> And then, when it go to my sister's bed, it will do that [hover]. And back again. And it was funny — where the hangers is, there is a hanger there and a hanger *there*, it wouldn't come across *at all*.
> I was wondering about that.
> And then it would go back again; I lose it, I get it, I lose it. When I think it's away I will get it again. And it go to Peggy's bed. She's giving me the sign that she was there.
> And that was funny. Ohhhh, I seen that myself.

Dónal told me another story of a time three years earlier when his sister was very ill, but eventually recovered. He was standing in the porch, which has a window on either side, waiting for the nurse to come to see Peggy who had woken that morning with a pain in her heart. 'When I looked over to the window, I seen a bird or something passing,' Dónal said. He looked quickly out the other window. A strange woman was going by, keeping close to the wall. 'Dark hair, and the hair was as deep as that, going onto the shoulder.' Dónal thought that she was about to walk around the side of the house, the gable end, but she did not appear. He went out. 'When I looked at the corner, she was getting as small as a doll. I seen her. And she went down in the foundation. She disappeared in the minute. And Peggy was all right after that. She lasted three years after that. And that was funny, too.'

* * *

Seán Ó hEochaidh told me about the 'gentle places', *áiteanna uaisle* in Irish. 'They were all over the countryside, the gentle spots. And these were supposed to be places that weren't to be touched by humans because the wee folk, or the gentle folk, or the fairies were supposed to live in these places or the surroundings.'

On Tory, the *áit uasal* was usually found along the coast. Walking along the cliffs, an islander would see something that tempted him: an ounce of tobacco out on the very edge of the cliff, or a very useful log near the rocks below, rolling in and out with the ocean swell. This was the method the fairies used to try to draw a human to his death when he came too close to their territory. Dónal knew of several instances of this kind.

> I heard about a friend of mine, and he's dead now. A cousin to me. Oh, he was telling everybody.
>
> And he rise in the morning and he went down to the gap to see if the sea is big. And the sea *was big*, did ye know.
>
> And when he look over at the side there — you know the other side of the rocks, going down — he see a big log, that's a timber, four foot square, *sixty* foot in length. A log.
>
> And when he went over to the place, there was no log *at all!*
>
> *Disappeared. No log at all!*
>
> And his uncle come over. I know his uncles. I know him, I know them all. His uncle says 'Did you get it?'
>
> 'No. I went over to the place and there was no log at all. That's funny. Disappeared.'
>
> And he went to bed that night, and he rise again in the morning. And he went down to the same place that he seen it before, to have a look over. And the log was there, in the morning again,
>
> *sixty* foot in length and *four foot square*, sitting at the rocks.
>
> And he went to the same place to *see*. *No log*. Oh, aye, he was telling me, and that was true. His uncle seen it too.
>
> And he done it *three times*. He went away out the third time and the log was there, and when he went *over* —

disappeared. 'Well, I will go the fourth time,' he says, 'I will do this.'

And the fourth time he rise in the morning and the log was there. He went over. The log disappeared.

He think to himself, '*That's* funny, that one'. He went down to the shore, searching round the beach. Did ye know what he get? A *cask* of whiskey. And that was funny now.

Look at the way they [the fairies] was drawing him over.

He got a big *thirty* gallon of whiskey,
and that was *funny*!

They say those that's dead is coming *back* again. They must come from the other world. They're not coming from *this* world. They're like *shadows*.

There is another world and some believe, some not. There is another world, and I know that. I *know*.

He got the barrel, thirty gallons of whiskey. And that's the way they draw him over. Give him a sight. They come from the other world,
and *that's* true.

He had a brother; there were *three* brothers. And one of them was lost on the boat.

And the two of them was away fishing and had no time, at the *harvest* time. There was no time to stook the corn. It was *tied*, tied up in sheaves on the ground, but they had no time to stook it, put it up. And the time was going by.

And this night — a moonlit night, the two of them was at home. The other brother was drowned. Buried.

And they start putting up the stooks, when one of them look over and saw the man that was drowned doing the same. He started at the other side of the field, putting the stooks.

And they was stooking the same, putting up, the two brothers who was alive and the man who was drowned doing the same.

> In the morning there was no stooks at all on the fairy side.
> Aye. Aye. They're only shadows. They can't do it, but they give you the sight, that's all. And the sheaves was lying in the field, the same. Sheaves of corn.
> And that was funny.

My visit to Dónal, on that rainy evening, passed quickly and as I left he assured me that he would 'think on' some more stories. The next time I stopped in to see him, with my tape recorder, I was surprised to discover that the first subject for my entertainment was none other than a character well known to me in my childhood, Will-o'-the-Wisp.

> And they will call here a man, called Willie-the-Wist. Did you ever hear about him? He's running with a candle.
> I heard my brother saying he was out with a crew for a cargo of turf, from the mainland, one time. And they didn't come home that day.
> And the people living out there seen this every night, a blue light going like a candle, going on the place where the bog was. And it will go in between the rickles.
> 'It's on the bog again tonight,' they would say, 'the light.'
> A *blue* light. And running here and running there. And they're saying it was a man called Willie-the-Wist. I don't know if this was true.
> I heard my brother say it. He was out that night. And that was funny.

Fairies, sometimes called leprechauns, are usually thought of as tricky little old men who, if caught, will reveal a pot of gold. Others are known to be shoemakers, the sound of whose hammers tapping on the soles of fairy shoes may be heard on a summer morning. The sound of hammer and nails that Dónal's father heard outside his door on the day his mother lay dying was made, it seems, by not quite so charming little fairies. As I was sitting in the front room of the house where the incident occurred, I felt a small shiver across my shoulders as Dónal spoke.

> Well. My father was telling me. His mother was laying in bed and she was — ah, she was dying away, did ye know. And he know it himself that she's to *die*.
> And he start out the door, to start making the coffin, and the hammers are going. My father was listening. And he went out.
> 'You may as well,' he says, 'quit *that*. We know ourselves that she is going to die.'
> Making a coffin outside, and *all* the houses around *heard* the noise. And that was funny. Eh? The *sound* only. Hammering the *nails*.
> *No coffin!*
> 'You may as well stop the noise', my father says, 'we know ourselves, that she's going to die.'

* * *

'That figure of a man is always there,' Kathleen Rodgers told me one evening when I mentioned the fairy at Portadoon. Patsy Dan joined in. 'They reckon, the community here reckons, that it's a very, very lonely place and that such a figure *is* there at all times. And he was supposed to have attacked someone from the island too, that was carrying a currach. Long, long ago. And that the man had to let the currach down and chase away himself to the East Village. Oh, they always say that. But may God give him rest if he is really there for *penance*. There's a number of people scattered around like that that have died on this earth, for that's the saying anyway, and that they're putting in their penance on very isolated lonely places.'

It may have seemed 'long long ago' to Patsy, a generation younger than Dónal, but to the older man it was not long ago at all.

> Well. I'm going to tell you another one. Another true, true.

I know the man and all from the east end, above Doonport [Portadoon]. Well that's the place it happened. There was supposed to be a fairy to be seen always there. That was true.

Well. This man, one time, money was scarce, there was nothing going here but the fishing.

And I heard him telling another man. We were sitting beside the fire — he had a wee boy and I will be over with *him* — I was listening.

'One day,' he says, 'I will take a notion to dig some limpets.' Limpets for bait, for the fish, did ye know. And there's a port there called Port Deilg, that's the place he went *out*, fishing.

He had three sisters and his mother, in the house; the rest was married, away.

And he was fishing at Deilg, Port Deilg you call it. And he count the fish in the currach and he had nine dozen. And he was making ready to go home.

And he didn't go in to Port Deilg, he made up to Doonport, to go in there. And he had, ye know, a wee currach. And they *all* on the island had the same.

And when he was going in, this man come over where the cliff's fell, out from the stones there.

And he was looking at him coming up. He would be able to catch the currach when the currach struck on the beach, to *help* him, did ye know.

Well, he was *thinking* that anyhow.

And he was a good size of a man, closing up to six foot in height. A dark complexion, dark like a foreigner.

And he was standing on the beach, looking at the fish in the currach. A fairy.

And the fisherman then pushed the currach out; he was feared to go in, did ye know. And the fairy went over and went in under the stones.

'I have a good chance now,' the fisherman said, 'to go in.'

He tried it again and when he was coming in again

the fairy come *over* again and at the place where the currach was touching the beach, he was standing there.

'Oh, Christ!' the fisherman pushed the currach out again.

And the fairy went over, under the stones again. His home was there.

And, 'Ah well I don't give a damn,' the fisherman says. 'I will go in the *third* time, no matter if he come or not.' He tried it again anyhow.

And when he was coming in to the beach, there was an anchor there of stone, with a line.

And it was close to the currach when he jump out. And he catched the stone, and he run with the line, up, up, up the beach. Run, and he didn't look behind him.

And he throw the stone like this, *away up* [on the cliff]. And leave the currach there on the beach.

And he went down home, to call his sisters to ask them to come along with him to bring the currach up. He had three sisters and his mother.

And the four went down, the three sisters and himself. They were strong too, did ye know, the three sisters. And they catch the currach, and leave the currach up at the grass, on the top.

And the fairy went over between the stones and the fisherman never seen him no more.

Was it funny the way it was, that it was sight always? Aye.

* * *

The last story Dónal told me is my favourite. It is also of interest to me because, although I had heard about 'good' and 'bad' black cats and had been told by Séamus Ó Catháin, the archivist of the Folklore Department at University College, Dublin, the fascinating tale of 'King of the Cats' and had read in books of mythology and folklore about people turning into animals, I do not remember hearing about a cat turning into a man.

Well, I'm going to tell you about a funny thing, a funny thing. Well, it was a ghost.

My mother and grandmother were stopping up there, above Patsy's house, in an old house that time, a *thatched* house.

And my grandmother had two daughters, Kathleen, one of them, and *my* mother, Grace. When that happened my mother was twelve year old, and the sister, Kathleen, ten. And the father was lost,
>drowned,
>>blown by the wind.

And the house was full of *mice*. Full. Ohhh, she was cursing on that, my mother. Oh, that is true, many's a time she was telling me, sitting there.

And they had no cat in the house, for keeping the mice away. My grandmother say with them, 'If we get a sense on a cat, will you take it in for the night, and keep it in?'

A couple of nights after that, a cat was *Eaou, eaou*, running on the ditches near the house.

'Oh!' my grandmother say with the daughters, 'Did ye hear the cat? Will ye go out to have a hunt on him?'

And the cat, *Eaou, eaou*.

And the three went out, the two daughters and the mother.

And they were tired, and when they try to catch the cat he will jump. He will jump, here, there and on the ditch, did ye know.

And they were tired, and when they try to catch the cat he will jump. He will jump, here, there and on the ditch, did ye know.

My grandmother was tired, and one of the daughters, the youngest daughter, she was ten years old, 'Ah, I'm tired!' An hour after him; and it was the same always. The *think* they will have it, like that, and it will jump.

But my mother follow him. My mother follow him and he went in in another field. Jumping in. And my mother was strong, and she wasn't heavy did ye know, and she followed the cat.

Ah, many's a time she was cursing about that.

And she followed the cat and she followed the cat. She showed me the place and all, my mother. And she followed the cat.

Ah! She was getting *tired*. All night after him. She fall and rise and fall, and her knees was all cut.

'Here's the last time now,' she says, 'I'm going to turn back home.' When she was going to catch him like that, he turned [into] a *man*.

Eh? Well, that's true as I'm going to die. My mother was cursing on him, sitting there.

And she knew the man and all on the island, the man was drowned too, Hughie Diver here, a man called Hughie Diver. *I* knew the people and all. I knew the brothers and all.

And that was funny. When she turned like that around, she was going to catch the cat and it turned a man. Ohh, Christ. A big man, six foot in height. And he was *laughing*. And that was funny. He was laughing.

And many's a time my mother was cursing on that man, Hughie *Diver* you call his name. My mother knew him. And he was drowned, too, and he was buried *years* ago, and that was funny. Eh?

Oh, that's true. I'm telling you. ■

Mary McClafferty
(b. 1915)

I seldom go to visit Mary. It is not that I would feel unwelcome, it is that I am afraid that I will interrupt her. Her early life was one of hard work and still, due perhaps to a combination of habit and necessity, she never seems to stop doing chores. We exchange a few words when I meet her on the way to the post office. When I see her taking a bucket of feed to the henhouse across the road from Eilish's, her flock of free-ranging brown hens and the elegant rooster jostling at her heels, squawking hungrily, I walk over and have a chat. I wave to her when I see her in the distance, gutting fish, or moving purposefully in the direction of the back of the house, carrying a large tin of whitewash and a paint brush. But I do not interrupt her, although I am tempted sometimes to do so. And so it is that I see Mary most frequently in working clothes, those that are appropriate to the particular task at hand. It is different, however, at the Sunday night *céilí*. There, in a pretty dress instead of a paint-flecked jumper, wearing light shoes instead of wellingtons (rubber boots), her hair not blown by Tory's strong winds, she is another person. And when she steps out onto the floor to dance, light as a feather, one can see her very clearly as she was when she went to Dublin to work many years ago, a pretty, auburn-haired girl of seventeen.

Mary had promised to do a tape for me about her childhood and married life. I came to her house one bright afternoon at four o'clock, just as she was finishing her dinner of herring and potatoes, in the back kitchen. We sat together until she was through; she then suggested we go into the kitchen. This was an invitation that no longer surprised me, as by now I was well acquainted with the old terminology for the modern sitting room. Mary lives in a low whitewashed house that sits by itself, several hundred yards back from the road, between Éamonn and Eilish Rodgers' and the school. It was built by Mary's husband Pádraig, when they left the old family house after the death of his parents. A patch of boggy meadow lies at the back, and the land beyond this, covered with rough grass, rises gently to the northern cliffs. Since 1978, when Pádraig himself died, Mary has been living here with her two unmarried sons and a grandson, in his twenties, whose family is on the mainland.

> My father had appendix when he died. And I was only a year and nine months at the time. And that was hard on my mother, *créatúr* [literally 'creature' — a sympathetic interjection], because William [the eldest] was eleven, that was all, and down from that. Well she got it tough, my mother.
>
> My mother's from Inishbofin, you know, and her brother, that's Éamonn, he was in Inishbofin at the time, and she had to take him in to help her. She had a horse and two cows, and a lot of land to set, and children and everything. And he stayed in seven months to help, after my father died.
>
> But my uncle was there at the time, that's Johnny Rodgers. He worked very hard too, you know: working with a horse that time, and putting out seaweed, and manure, and working at land and ploughing. [There were] a few, just a few slide-cars [carts with iron shod runners], at the time. In our house there was a big [wheeled] cart for the horse and Lord, a *thaisce*, we worked hard in our days. There was no such thing as coal, no mainland turf, just our own turf.
>
> But we still and all managed.
>
> Una was nine, and John, God rest him, and Dan and me were at school together. William had to leave school when he was twelve. He was cutting corn at twelve years.
>
> When I was around ten year old we would be at school in the morning from half nine till four o'clock.

So then after school we would just do our homework, the whole of us together, one here and one there.

We had sums, English *and* Irish; and geography, and grammar, diction, transcription.

And we were learning, that time, catechism as well. In my time you had to learn a lot of catechism. But that's gone now.

And my mother would be out working; she was always out there, the *créatúr*, to work. She *had* to do it.

Well, when that [homework] was finished, I would just go for a bucket of water and I would clean the floor and wash the dishes. And I would make a scone of bread — at that age! And make beds. I would go over then to the byre, and I would clean under the horse and the cows, and clean all around the byre.

And my mother had varicose veins and when she come over from the fields they were so *sore*.

Créatur, she had a poor time.

Since she died, why I think on her, ye know, once I'm up in age myself. She suffered a lot. But still I was a good help to her, and Una was. And John, God rest him, and Dan, they were fishing.

Well, William was only eighteen, when he went to fish. Herrings.

He fell down from the cliffs, up here. He got his arm broke.

And I was there when he fell. I was *there* when he fell, the *créatúr*.

My mother was over in the field and I got ready the tea [for the fishermen] in the evening; I went up with all the girls at that time. All the boats was fishing, round about eleven boats was fishing, d'ye know, oars. They had a few engines, not very much. Mickey Mooney's motor that time and McGinty's motor, that was the only two boats there was, taking the fish out to the country, over to Kincasslagh and down to Downings.

So I was there, just at tea, when the boat came in. Mickey Mooney's, d'ye know, a small boat, but there was an engine in it. And he came in with it as far as the rocks.

And William, the *créatúr*, he jumped out, and where he was trying to go up the cliff, Dorothy, you *couldn't* dream that anybody on earth would go over that way. And just, nothing I seen but he put the hand on the stone and the stone came with him and *down* he went,

down he went to the *sea*.

But there was another rock come down beside him and when *he* went down in the sea he put his arm like this, and the rock came. On his arm.

I had nothing to see but *all* blood.

Lord, I'll never forget that day.

I was just round about twelve years that time, that was all.

And Mickey Mooney shouted up to me — there was nobody there but me. But Dan was coming over with the cow, putting it over, away from the cliffs. And when he heard me squeal, 'Good Lord,' he says to me, 'What's wrong?'

'Oh,' says I, 'William fell from the cliffs.'

I came down home, and there was nobody there but my uncle. And *he* was in bed in the kitchen; at that time there was a bed in the kitchen in every house.

I went in at the door and I was crying and crying. And he had no eyesight, the old man my uncle. He was, *créatúr*, in bed and he was singing; and I went in crying.

'Oh, is that you, Mary?'

'Yes.'

'What's wrong with you, a *thaisce*, what's wrong with you?'

'Ah, William,' says I, 'fell from the cliffs.'

Créatúr, he came out. I don't know how he went; but I went over the road, and my mother was over working the potatoes.

And, oh Lord, I was crying. *She* was down in the field. She shouted up to me, 'Mary, what's wrong with you?'

'Ah, says I, 'William fell from the cliffs.'

'William fell from the. . .?'

'Yes. He fell from the cliffs, mother. From the cliffs.'

'Is he dead there, or what's wrong?'

'Well, his arm's hurt anyhow.'

Créatúr, she just came out to the ditch, ye know, she walked over with *me*.

At that time, Dorothy, the people were very nice. And if anything would happen to anybody they would sit there, *helping* you. And that night the house was full; old people, young people, till morning.

None of us went to bed that night.

And my mother went out in the morning to the mainland. And she went up to Letterkenny [hospital]. And many a time I heard her talking, *créatúr*. She went in, she says to me, and he was in bed with his arm off.

He was there three weeks, Lord, when he came home. And after coming home then, he wasn't able to do anything. And he *hadn't a penny, créatúr*, he wasn't able to earn a penny. And he wasn't able to get disability or dole or nothing.

And then it was Mrs Shiels, that was here, she gave him a job in her shop. William was working with her, helping her in the shop. And then when he was six or seven years there, she gave him thirty pounds. And that's how he started in the shop, and he got on all right, thank God.

* * *

When I was then round thirteen, I went then out to the mainland myself. I had to go. I was working out there for a year, working on a farm. And when I went out first, I hadn't much sense.

In the morning I would have to get up, round about five o'clock. And take out three cows. And see to them till one. Without just a cup of tea in the morning, nothing else. And she [the mistress] had plenty of food, plenty of money, but still she wasn't good to the servant girls, ye know.

So, when the first morning I got out at five o'clock, she gave me a wee cup, a pint cup, and she says to me, '*Come on out,*' she says to me, 'you have to try and milk the cow.'

I went out with her to the byre. And when she had the two other cows milked, I had only one pint of milk in the tin.

I was there for seven months. When the seven months was in, I was able to milk the three. And I *had* to milk the three.

I was working at land. I was putting out seaweed. I was putting in manure. I was cleaning the byre. I was washing.

And I was washing sheets and quilts and everything in the house at *that* age. And the *sweat* coming *down,* just as if you threw water on me.

Well, I was threshing corn, with a machine. Threshing corn.

There was a man there in the house, and he made a machine for threshing corn. Well, I would go into that barn in the morning — many a time I think on that too — and *he* would put in the corn like this, and I had the handle the whole day.

And, if I would get plenty to eat at that time, but I didn't. Just, when I would come in she gave me two potatoes, and maybe a herring. But there was no such thing as leaving anything for me. I had to go on with that. And at that time, at that *age* — I was up early, ye know — if she would leave me a pot of potatoes, I would take the whole pot of potatoes.

And, do you know what she would give me in the morning? She would give me a herring, fried overnight, with a cup of tea. And she had a sideboard here, in the kitchen, and there was three plates of butter in there!

Oh, she wasn't good.

But I was there seven months, that's till November. And she told me then to stay for another while; I was there for a year. I came in home to see my mother and I had nothing in my hand but three pounds. That's the only wages she gave me. *Three* pounds.

I was *working* at everything; washing dishes, sweeping floors, going to the shop, putting out turf with creels on my back; my back was all cut. I was putting out the cattle twice a day, I was milking three in the morning and milking three in the evening. Tsk, tsk, tsk. I couldn't tell you all I was doing.

I had a wee room down here, where I was sleeping. And there was nothing there on the wall but all snails. White snails on the wall.

And I was so tired at night, d'ye you know what I would do? I would take a cardboard box, and I would take the lid off. And I would put them like this from the wall, in the cardboard box. And I would leave the box under the bed overnight.

And sure they would come out of the box too. But *I hadn't the sense.*

And when I would wake now in the morning again — you know the white track they leave on the fields? That track was all on my quilt where I was lying in the morning. Wasn't that terrible?

And on Sundays the same thing. Hens and ducks and geese and everything like that. I hadn't a minute.

I was completely overwhelmed by the thought of all the work that poor, small girl had to do, day after day. 'I suppose she had to let you go to Mass, at least,' I said. 'Wait till I tell you this,' Mary laughed. '*Good Lord.*'

I left one morning for Mass at nine o'clock. If she would leave me go on the road, if she would say to me, 'Walk over, Mary, to the chapel, walk over just, walk over the road.' But she would send me to the cliffs and down on the other side [a short cut]. And I wasn't used to that, d'ye know, I had no sense.

But this Sunday I left for Mass. Tsk, tsk. *Good Lord.*

And when I was up on top of the cliffs, here comes the fog.

And I didn't know where I was. But I kept on going and going and I didn't know where I was going until I came to a big lake.

I *came* to this big lake — I could be drowned too — and I stood, looking in the water, and I said to myself, 'That's funny, where I am. I'd better,' I said to myself, 'go back again.'

Good Lord. Twelve years old. I could go someplace that I would be lost.

I went back again, looking before me, at the sods and everything and the cliffs way over. And I was walking from nine till twelve. I was the whole morning astray.

I came out then back at Dixon's. My aunt she lived there, she was married out there. And wasn't I silly, Dorothy, after knowing she was there, I never let on anything. At that time that was the way we were going.

And she came out the door and she walked over to me and she said to me, 'Where did you come from? Where did you come, a *thaisce*?'

'Oh, I was going to Mass, and I'm too late.' That's all I said.

And when I left the house she gave me a shilling — that's five pence now — and she said to me, 'On your way, Mary,' she says, 'coming home, have a pound of rice with you.'

I walked over to Gortahork — I was great too ye know.

I went into the shop then and I got a pound of rice; and I went over then with some of the Meenacladagh people — that's over this direction.

They told me, 'You'd better come over with us.' They knew me some way. 'And come over the road,' they said to me, 'because it's very foggy,' they said, 'you might be lost.'

I went over anyway with them, I came down by the road and come home. I had a new pair of shoes on, that my mother sent out to me — and the *half sole* came off, down to that, after the walk!

And do you know when I came in, 'Why,' she says to me, 'did you come over the road? Why didn't you,' she said, 'take the short cut?'

'Well,' says I, 'it was foggy.' I never told her that I wasn't at Mass, I never told her *anything* about that. At that time, Dorothy, you would be afraid to say anything, she would scold me. I just walked in.

But, I had work to do. When I came in home then, to Tory, all I had with me was three pounds. That was all. I gave the three pounds to my mother and she just, *créatúr*, walked over the road with it into Ellie Ward's shop; she gave the three pounds to Miss Ward.

There was no money at the time. We had to put out sea-rods, and seaweed as well. The same year William lost his arm he was over with us, Dorothy, over to the shore putting out sea-rods. And me and John and Una.

At that time they would burn them, not the way they do now. Just put them in a big square with stones and burn the sea-rods and the seaweed together, and put them in bags. That's what we call kelp.

Well that year William lost his arm we got, I think, twelve pounds a ton, and that was very good at the time. We had five tons that year, but that was only thirty six pounds. The way they are now, you know, the money, thank God, is plentiful.

But not in my time.

* * *

When Mary was a child, the family lived in a 'tin house' (a house with a tin roof) on the site where William Rodgers' house and shop now stand. After the tin became rusty, felt was put over it, 'That's the kind of house we had.' Later, William got a grant from the Congested Districts Board and the family themselves 'broke out the old house', cleaned the stones and built it up again. 'William, and Dan, John and me and Una, putting out cement, putting up gravel, we build up that house.'

There are two things about the old place that Mary remembers well: the sound of the rain on the tin roof and the big white house. There was a small byre for the two cows, but the horse was kept in the kitchen. 'In the *kitchen*. There was a wall going over this direction and a door just there. And the *horse* was down there.' Their mother was usually out working, so there were many times when the children were alone in the house, either before or after school. And a big white horse would walk in the kitchen door. Frightened, they would all go 'up the room'. One day when the horse had come into the kitchen, 'who passed down but the priest. I remember that priest well, Father Sweeney from Fanad, and I was only young, I wasn't at school at that time.' The priest had seen the horse enter the house and so came in himself. 'We were up in the room,' Mary told me, 'I don't know did we say anything at all. It was him that put out the horse from the door.' In those days, children never spoke to the priest unless he spoke to them first.

> That's the teaching we got. We could never speak to him.
>
> And my mother would say to us, 'Never,' she says,' never speak to the priest unless' — Lord save us, there's a good change in the people too, a good change — 'Don't speak now to the priest, none of you now, *unless* he speaks first. You can answer him,' she says, '*then*.'
>
> And when he was going round then with the sacraments she would say, 'Now, when you're passing now over, for God's sake now, don't speak to the priest.'
>
> And she'd tell us then *why*.
>
> And when you would be at school, if we would see the priest coming, we would run to the door and we'd open the door for the priest. And whoever would be out on the edge of the street, when the priest would be leaving, we would get up and open the door and let him out. But there's no such thing as that now.

Mary was seventeen when she left Tory again to work on the mainland. This time she went to Dublin; and she and her good friend Bríd Carroll, along with Tadhg McGinley, who was 'running the mails that time'. One of the lighthouse keepers accompanied them to Dublin; after that Mary was on her own. 'I spent a year there — ah, *a thaisce*, I had a terrible time.'

> When *I* left home I thought I had nothing to do but just walk into the work. And people, elderly people, would come in and say to me, 'Mary, are you going away tomorrow?'
> 'Yes.'
> 'Have you got a job in Dublin?'
> 'Oh, the job is there and the office is there.' That's what I would say. I had no *sense*. Seventeen.
> But I have now.
> So, we went up to Dublin anyway, and I know rightly I was staying with Mrs Downs. It was a kind of hostel.
> This morning I got up and I went to the office, walking, *walking*. And I didn't know on God's earth *where* I was going. Just I would see a guard [policeman] here now and again to ask him was I on the right road.
> I went into this office, and I took the information to the woman there. 'Well,' she says to me, 'there's a lady,' she says, 'out in Whitehall, looking,' she says, 'for a maid. For housework.'
> Well, I thought I had nothing to do but walk in to that lady. Lord Almighty. There was a strike at that time, on the trams. And she told me that.
> 'Well,' says I, 'Have I now to walk out to Whitehall?'
> 'Oh, yes,' she says. 'Will you,' she says to me, 'will you be able to manage?'
> 'Sure rightly I will. Well,' says I, 'I'll do my best anyway,' says I.
> And I had this note with me, a wee piece of paper with something written on it. I walked out anyhow. And I was walking and walking till I was dead out,
> trying to get to Whitehall.
> But Dublin was nice at that time. You could walk at two o'clock at night in Dublin that time; but not now,

they say anyway. But I walked and walked. And I would meet an elderly woman or meet a man, no matter *who* I would meet, I would ask them, 'Am I on the right road to Whitehall?' And that's the way I got to the door.

So the lady opened the door, and I says to her, 'Are you looking for a maid?' says I. 'I was told that you were looking for a maid and I came so far, to see.'

'Well,' she says, 'I got the maid,' she says, 'this morning.'

'Well,' says I, 'that's all right.'

'Well,' I said to myself. 'Good Lord Almighty, what do I do.' And I walked anyway till I came to the hostel again. Whatever way I came through I don't know. And I stayed with Mrs Downs overnight again.

But I got up the following morning, and I went in [to the agency] again and she says to me. 'There was a lady here,' she says, 'wanting a maid,' she says. 'Mrs Downey,' she says, 'from Dalkey Avenue.'

I remember it well.

'Will you try it?' she says. 'Will you be able to manage to Dalkey Avenue?'

'Well,' says I, 'I'll do my best.' *Again.*

I went the same direction, but I hadn't as much to go anyhow. And do you know, I was killed out in that house. I got a job with her; but still and all *I couldn't tell* you. D'ye know how I would go upstairs at night? Pulling myself up on the steps.

I would have to do washing on Monday, washing everything on earth on Monday. On Tuesday I would have to iron all these things. There was three rooms upstairs and a bathroom. They had a room, even itself, for shoes and for clothes. I had to see to upstairs on Wednesday, polish and clean. And then the bathroom and the stairs.

And down below then there was a sitting room, a dining room and a drawing room. A big, big house. And every morning I would get up I had to open up the windows, there were shutters inside. And the chain on the door even, I had to polish. And then on Saturday I would have to clean the chimney.

Clean the chimney. And only one pound a month.

I had to clean the chimney, and polish the chimney, and sure I would be as black as tar when I was finished. And cleaning the railings and polishing and after that done, cleaning all round. I had to take off the clothes I wore, wash my hands, start and clean all round the kitchen, till one o'clock at night.

And I wasn't long there till she had a baby. I was one night after going to bed, just going to rest myself when she walked in — oh, Lord Almighty, sure I got a terrible time. And she said to me, 'There's a jar,' she says, 'for outside,' she says, 'on the table and it's not washed properly at all. Come on out,' she says to me, 'come on out of bed.'

I had to get out of bed, and go out to the kitchen and wash the jar. And I had to get up at half five in the morning, and make a bottle for the child. Wasn't that poor?

But there was another one in the house. Maybe she was a friend [relation], or something. But she wasn't long there. She wasn't doing anything anyhow.

And she had a daughter as well. Mabel they called the daughter, and I had to call her 'Miss Mabel'. [Mary laughed.] But, a *thaisce*, wait till I tell you.

Oh, *Good Lord*. As far as I know, she was engaged to a man from Llandudno [in Wales]. I seen the man and all. And he would visit her every other weekend, and then she would go back the second weekend, herself and the mother.

But, this morning I got up quarter to seven, and I had no matches. And the boiler had to be warmed for the husband, to get up and get washed and a bath.

So he [the fiancé] was lying in one of the rooms, and the daughter and the mother was in another room. But I didn't think anything of that, ye know. I went to his door, at quarter to seven, and I knocked the door, a little. And says I to him, 'Have you got a match?'

'Yes, Mary,' he says. He knew me well, ye know, that was working there. He just put out his hand and he gave me the match. That was all. And I lit the fire.

But he must have told them. *A thaisce*, I got a terrible time over it. They nearly killed me;

they nearly, a *thaisce*, killed me for doing this.

I would say that the mother thought I was fond of him. After I came home I would be thinking on things like that, but not at the time.

And one morning I was upstairs before going to Mass, and here she [Mabel's mother] comes in. And she was putting in curls in her hair, like this; they were Protestants, ye know. She was putting in curls in her hair like this, with papers she had. And she says to me — Oh, Lord, I don't know; sure they could have killed me too, ye know; because they were against me. I noticed straight on, and they were a whole bunch together, they were all alike.

And the house was in a place where there was nobody there. There was just flowers all around, and there was nobody else near me. But, I was young at the time and I was strong, I suppose that's it.

She said to me this morning I was going to Mass, 'What's the reason,' she says to me, and she's putting in curls, 'what's the reason,' she says to me, 'that you were in that man's room in the morning?'

Well, if you said that to me now, I would faint. But says I, 'I *wasn't* in his room. I wasn't,' says I, 'in his room at all, in the morning. Sure,' says I, 'I went to the door and knocked the door and I asked for matches. Sure, that's nothing.' *A thaisce*, she started.

She started. 'Oh,' she said, 'it's no wonder,' she says, 'about the Catholics,' she says, 'no wonder,' she says,' about the Catholics. See,' she says to me, 'the Arranmore disaster?' [Twenty-one young people were drowned when the boat in which they were returning from the mainland after 'hooking' (gathering) potatoes in Scotland capsized.] That was the first day I heard about it. 'After,' she says, 'the priest collecting the money for them around here,' she says, 'sure it was a *Protestant* man, a Protestant,' she says, 'that give it all round.'

'Well,' says I to her, 'sure, I don't know anything about that.' *A thaisce*, she started. And they had that [religion] always on their mind, day and night. And many a time I think they could kill me, Dorothy, and nobody on God's earth would know what happened. And I would say she was jealous with me, too. When I was seventeen, you know, I was good-looking.

And I came in this one evening. I got ready a cup of tea for myself and when I walk upstairs, 'Come on in here to the room, Mary,' she says, 'my daughter's not well since you left.'

'What's happened?' says I. I sat down there at the fire. 'What's happened?'

'Oh,' she says, 'she had to get her mouth cut inside. The doctor was in and I think,' she says, 'that she has to go to the hospital.'

She says to me then, 'What do *you* do?' she says to me, 'on the island, if anything like this would happen?'

'Ah, well,' says I — I wasn't thinking on anything — 'the way we are, Missus,' I says, 'there's a priest there on the island and a nurse, and if anything happens we get the priest.'

'Hah!' she says, 'the *priest*,' she says, 'the priest!' [Mary laughed.] '*Good Lord*, 'she says to me — oh she was very cross — 'sure the priest is not able to make an operation now just like for Mabel here.'

'Well,' says I, 'we have an interest in the priest, and we think when he comes to the house' — and I was looking, she was very cross — 'we think,' says I, 'when he comes to the house that when he will see you that you'll be all right. That's the teaching,' says I, 'I got.'

'Ah, damn nonsense,' she says.

> But in my own mind I said to myself, 'I had better go to bed.'
> Then I came home at Christmas. And when I would leave she said to me, 'Mary,' she says, 'I'll give you any wages, if you stay.' I was a good working woman at the time. But I never went back.
> I got enough of it.

The recording on both sides of the tape went quickly with no interruptions. When I returned to Mary's house the next afternoon, we continued with the story of her life. After her marriage to Pádraig McClafferty, she remained with her mother, a custom that was prevalent in those days. Mary explained, as had her brother Dan, that staying on in the family house was due in large part to the fact that there was no money for the newly married couple to build a house for themselves. But there were other reasons as well. Sometimes either the husband or the wife was quite content in the old house and did not want to leave. And there were women who wouldn't, or couldn't, live with their mothers-in-law. 'It was very hard to please people at that time. Ah, they wouldn't take you in.' One man married only for the dole his wife would bring; there was no need to live with her. And the intricacies of the inheritance of land no doubt caused some difficulties. Mary gave a litany of examples:

> Aye. Look at Dan McClafferty. He was married to Kitty Doohan and *she* was at home all the time.
> And Jimmy Doohan was married to Mary McClafferty, and *he* was at home.
> And Johnny Doohan was married and he was at home. Three, in one house. That's true.
> And the McGinleys over here now, next to Jimmy Antoin, there was a crowd there married:
> Mary was married to Dan Mooney,
> and Nellie was married to Pat McClafferty,
> and Pádraig was married to Bríd Duggan, Bríd Antoin,
> and Dennis was married to Kitty Meenan...
> But that's the way they were here. And, Dorothy, that's

what left Tory without population. All of them that got married that time, they had no family. That generation left Tory without people.

And I had then to stay at home too, and I was working hard and I had to see to the child. I was six years at home before I came over down here with Patrick. And I had only John Joe at the time. John Joe was born in 1937 and Mary not born until 1942. If you would be married, at home, the old people — my mother and every other mother — they wouldn't allow you to have any more children. They had their own family and that was enough. And far too much sometimes; at that time there was six or seven of a family in every house.

Mary told me how hard the women had to work during their pregnancies. She herself, while pregnant, was 'working like a horse at the land': putting up hay on the carts in the harvest time; digging limpet; putting out seaweed, filling the creels with it and loading it into the cart; and filling carts with manure and putting it on the land.

The labour, before the baby was delivered, was often long, but it was taken for granted. 'It *has* to be that way,' Mary's mother would tell her. 'It has to be.' After the birth only oatmeal porridge and oatmeal bread was allowed. 'No such things as potatoes or meat,' Mary said. 'Oh! If anybody would go in with a cup of tea to you, with the home-made bread, my mother would murder them.'

It was Nurse McVeagh, one of a series of Public Health nurses on Tory, who delivered John Joe, Mary's oldest child, and many other children as well. She spent seventeen years on Tory and was remembered with great affection. 'She came to Tory round about 1936,' said Mary, 'when I got married. She was very old when she came here, the *créatúr*, but still and all. Ah, she was very good, Nurse McVeagh. She was a nice woman, she would do her best, *a thaisce*, that's the kind she was.'

Bridget Doohan told me that Nurse McVeagh would arrive for a delivery carrying a black bag in which were a pair of old shoes and two pairs of rubber gloves. She would leave the gloves in the bag and throw the shoes under the bed for luck. 'All the same it went on grand,' as Bridget remarked of her own delivery.

Gráinne Joe Rodgers said that Nurse McVeagh, after throwing the old shoes under the bed at the start, did nothing else but pray, holding her rosary beads hidden in her hand. All, however, were in agreement that she was 'great at cutting the cord'. Mary said: 'The best thing of all I seen her doing was the cord. She was very good at the cord and she was very good at the afterbirth. For I *know* that.'

When Nurse McVeagh retired, a nurse of a different type — according to Mary — took her place.

> When Paidí [Mary's third child] was born, there was a nurse here.
>
> Well, I'll tell you this story now.
>
> This Sunday she came down to me, down here, that was the seventeenth of March. And the first thing she said to me — I was gutting fish, at the door — she said to me, 'Mary, isn't it funny,' she says to me, 'the way the Tory people,' she says to me, 'keep their children a long time.'
>
> 'Isn't it funny, Mary,' *at the door*, she said this.
>
> 'Well,' I says to her, 'You have to wait anyhow.' Says I to her, 'Good Lord, nurse,' says I, 'we have to wait. Sure, I can't pull the child out of my stomach,' says I.
>
> 'Well,' she says. 'I notice that,' she says, 'the Tory people, the *way* they keep their children. And they're very slow, when they get sick as well.'
>
> 'Well,' says I, 'surely everybody has to wait here,' says I.
>
> 'Well,' she says, 'I hope you won't go over this day, anyhow.'
>
> *Sure* I was only due. But let me tell you this.
>
> This was on Sunday. And there was a drama over in this [building] — where the factory is, now — there was a drama there, *Paidí Michael Art*. It was a drama, Father McDyer had. And, God rest him, Pádraig was there too.
>
> And, round about seven o'clock in the evening, I was

in bed. But not a word out of me, you didn't say a *word*. There was no use in talking.

But that night, when the drama was over, Pádraig walked in, and I was in bed. 'Mary,' he says to me, 'are you not well?'

'No,' says I, 'but I'm all right,' says I, 'sure, I'm only starting. Maybe it will be morning,' says I 'before this'll happen.'

And I had the old people that time [Pádraig's parents] as well; the two of them, Barney, *his* father, and Nabla, *his* mother. And *she* was doting [senile], the woman.

But, he came in and this is what he said to me, 'Well,' he said to me, 'I'll let the priest know,' he says, 'about you.' And he says, 'He'll read you,' he says, 'an office anyhow, before you go to bed.'

I says, 'That will be all right.'

He went up to Father McDyer; and Father McDyer came in to me and I was out of bed again. And 'Mary,' he says — the old lady was talking, going strong in the room, she was doting — 'It will be all right, Mary,' he says. 'That child, Mary,' he says to me, 'will be born round about tomorrow morning,' he says, 'nine o'clock, when I'm reading the Mass.'

'Well,' I says to myself, I didn't say that to the priest, but says I to myself, 'If I have to suffer until nine o'clock tomorrow morning…'

This is what he said, 'And don't worry, Mary,' he says, 'you'll be all right.'

But, Dorothy, the shape I was in. Paidí was born at nine o'clock in the morning as the priest said.

So the nurse came over round about eight or half eight, and do you know what? She nearly took my life. And do you know what she did?

The child was born and she wasn't able to do anything with the afterbirth. And *the sea* was *mad* high. And it was clear ten [force ten winds]. That was the seventeenth of March. She came in and she says to

Pádraig, 'No trawler or nothing,' she says, 'will be able to come today?'

'Oh, no,' Pádraig says.

'I can't do nothing about this woman,' she says, 'I can't do nothing about her.'

Jennie Hughie, that time, she was August-born. And she got the doctor for *her*. That day was good...

She wasn't able to do anything.

So she said to me, *again*, 'It's funny, Mary,' she says — she had the child all right, and the cord, I done all the rest myself — it's funny how the Tory people,' she says, 'keep the afterbirth.' [Mary laughed.]

'But, good Lord, nurse,' says I to her and I was lying in bed, 'Good Lord, nurse,' says I, 'when Nurse McVeagh was here,' says I, 'and she was only an *old woman*. And she could get the afterbirth,' says I, 'just put her finger there,' says I, 'and the afterbirth would come. I suppose,' says I, 'you never done anything like this before?'

'Ah, no,' she says, 'it's the Tory people themselves, she says, 'is the cause of this.'

But wait till I tell you *this*. That was all right.

'Well,' she says, 'wait,' she says, 'I'll go up home yet,' she says, 'and I'll get my husband's dinner,' she says, 'and when I come back again,' she says, 'you might be all right.' Paidí was born at nine o'clock and this is two o'clock nearly. That was bad.

'Well,' says I, 'by the way *you're* going,' says I, 'I won't be all right today.'

She came over then when she gave him the dinner; she came over and she *must* have [had] a drink because she went over to me,

and she couldn't do nothing.

She opened this case. And she took out a bottle about that size. And what was written on the bottle? 'Poison!'

That's true. And if there was a woman there that wouldn't be able to read, she would be dead. I'll tell you why she was going to do this. She knew rightly if that [afterbirth] wouldn't come that I would die. And, she thought to herself, 'I'll try this anyway. If she *dies, nobody* will *know* what happened.' That's as true as God. I told that to Father McDyer too, when he came down.

She came over with this bottle, and she opened the door and she said to Pádraig, 'Have you an egg cup?'

The *créatúr*, her give her an egg cup, but still I was looking at the bottle. And she put *this* wee bottle, about that size, in the egg cup. 'Here, Mary,' she says to me, '*drink* this,' she says to me, 'it will do you all the good in the world.'

'Well, nurse,' says I, 'I never took poison in my life.' I was great too, Dorothy.

'I had *no* call, nurse,' says I, 'to take poison. Because,' says I, 'when Nurse McVeagh was here,' says I, 'she never gave me the like of that.'

'Well,' she says, 'you can have it,' she says to me, 'anyhow.'

'No,' says I, 'I won't. Put that back,' says I, 'where you got it.'

Well here, she put it back in the bottle again, she put on the top, she put it in the case, and away she goes, up to the priest. She never told the priest that she gave me this bottle, she told the priest that I wasn't well yet.

But he says to her — 'Leave that woman,' he says, 'alone for another hour. Don't go near her,' he says, 'that woman will be all right when I'll go down.'

He came down to me — Father McDyer, a big tall man — and he opened the door over. And I was as strong, that time, Dorothy, as a horse.

'Mary,' he says to me, 'congratulations.' This is the first time ever I hear 'congratulations'.

'Congratulations, Mary,' he says, 'you're all right, *a thaisce*.' He was very good to me. He could see the way I was going.

'But, Father,' says I, 'I'm not well yet at all,' says I.

'I know,' he says, 'you're not.'

'And wait till I tell you this,' says I. 'But sure,' says I,

> 'half an hour ago and the nurse took over a wee bottle here of poison and put it in an egg cup and giving it to *me*.'
>
> 'She *what?*' he says.
>
> 'I know rightly, Father, what happened. She thought that I would die with this anyhow, with the complaint I had, and then if I would take that, Father, I would be dead now.'
>
> '*Good Lord,*' he says to me, 'is that right?'
>
> 'Oh, yes, Father.'
>
> 'Well,' he says to me — he went over on the bed with me, put his hand on my head [and made the sign of the cross] — he was very good that priest, too. And he said to me, 'You'll be all right now, Mary,' he says, 'in an hour's time.' But he says, 'If you'll get someone,' he says, 'that will be up in ages, they might know all about it.'

Fortunately for Mary, Nelly Rodgers Cormac came in. She heated a piece of flannel in the big pot of boiling water she brought to the bedside, and applied it to Mary's abdomen, repeating this treatment for half an hour.

> That afterbirth, Dorothy, came with no bother. Well, I suppose that that did it, but the priest done his best for me.
>
> And my mother that time was out on the road, *créatúr*. And they were saying that she was over and back and over and back, doing this [wringing her hands].
>
> The day was rough.

Mary was married at twenty-two, but continued to live with her mother for six years. Then she moved into the house of her husband's parents; not the one she lives in now but an old, two-storied dwelling just west of Ward's hotel. It was very damp, there were leaks in the kitchen window and there was no cement on the porch floor, only clay. On the mornings when the priest was coming to bring the sacraments to the old people, Mary would pray for the rain to stop and the sun to come out. For while it

rained the porch was very muddy. She would watch intently for
the arrival of the priest. 'I would see the priest coming down, I
would have a dry bag, and just put the bag under the priest's
feet, coming in the door.'

Mary had worse things than leaks to worry about; as she said
to me, 'Well *a thaisce*, I had a time there. It was bad enough at
home, but my brothers were there and my mother was there and
we'd potatoes and milk and hens. But now when I went out on
my own, with *them* [Pádraig's parents], I had nothing at all. And
the old lady was doting for three years. And I couldn't tell you all
I done with *her*.' The old lady must have had what is now known
as Alzheimer's disease, for not only was she senile but she was
belligerent as well, scratching Mary's eyes and pulling her hair
while her daughter-in-law was trying to wash her, or put her to
bed, or get her dressed in the morning. Although she was blind,
she would stray from the house at any time of the day or night
and Mary and Pádraig would have to go out and bring her back.
And constantly she cursed and swore and sang. Mary told me of
a rather surprising thing that happened during the time Pádraig
was working in England.

> And God rest Pádraig, he left, himself and Eoghan
> Whoriskey, that's Dan's wife's brother. They went over to
> England; at that time he had to. He was there working
> and he only had four pounds a week. That's all he had.
>
> So the morning he left, the priest was going round
> with the sacraments, on the old people. Well Pádraig,
> God rest him, left at half eight with Johnny Dixon's boat,
> and the priest came round about eleven. That was the
> first start with him, Father McGonigle, who was after
> coming to Tory that time. And he was a young priest and
> he had no Irish.
>
> And I went down to the room and I asked the old lady
> would she get up, that the priest would soon be here;
> and she wouldn't get up for me. But, says I, 'I'll do my
> best,' I says, 'to dress you in bed.'
>
> 'Oh, no,' she says. She would put her fingers in my
> eyes, my hair and everything. I was all cut. So I left her

just as she was, and you know yourself how she was, at that time, poor clothes, Dorothy, and everything.

That was the *first* morning I spoke to a priest and he had the sacraments with him.

So at the door just, *créatúr*, when he was coming in. 'Father,' says I, 'I'm very sorry,' says I, 'I have to speak to you. About the old lady, she's not well, and she won't dress herself, Father, and she won't get up with me to the fire. And before,' says I, 'you go any further, Father,' says I, 'come down to the room till you see her.'

He came down with me to the room. And he stood at the bed just.

And he was listening to her. Cursing. Swearing. Talking. And singing like hell.

'Well, Mary,' he said to me, 'I'm very sorry about you,' he says. 'You have a bit of trouble. But I can't give her,' he says, 'the sacraments because she'd throw them out. And she's better off,' he says, 'the way she is.'

Well, that was all right.

Pádraig, he was away for five months. I had to send for him, the last time. I had too much to do. I had two cows. And I was working the land. Una and my brother John, they would come over to help me. And Willy Dooley, God rest him, in the east end. Setting potatoes and digging potatoes and everything, on my own. And that old lady, you know; I was afraid always that the old lady would fall out of bed or stray. That was the worst thing on *me*.

I would have to go for turf to the cliffs. We had no mainland turf. And we had no coal. Just the turf we dig ourselves.

So, *this* day I went in to Father McGonigle, and this was a miracle anyway. *I* know it myself.

I went in to the door and I had only with me twenty-five pence. For Mass. That was all I had to give him.

I stood at the door and says I to him, 'Father,' says I. 'I'm going to tell you this now about the old lady. *I'm* there as a stranger, I'm married to her son. And *her* daughter,' says I, 'is over working with Miss Ward. And the worst thing of all, Father,' says I, 'the way it is, Father, now. I have to go here and there, I have to go to the shop, I have to go for turf, I have to go to the field. And if anything happens to her, Father, when I'm away, I won't be able to take that. It's all right, Father, if the *daughter* was in the house, but she's not there, and I'm a strange woman. And what'll they say to *me*?'

'And, Pádraig,' says I, 'is away today,' says I.

'Is he gone?' he said.

'Yes. He has to go, Father. Sure there's no money. He had to go to earn for the children.'

'Well,' he says, 'I'll do my best for you, Mary,' he says.

Isn't it *funny*. From *that* day, till the *day* he [Pádraig] marched in the house — she didn't say a word. From *that* day I was talking to the priest. And I only gave him twenty-five pence, to remember her in Mass.

At twelve o'clock at night, before that, she was through the house, and throwing water, I couldn't tell you all she was doing.

But since that day Pádraig left, till the *day* he came back, she was all right.

And do you know the *day* he came back, *that night*, she was on the go again.

Oh that's true as God, as true as I'm telling you.

* * *

Mary said that there were many old, damp houses on Tory when she was young, but that the one she lived in when she first went to live with Pádraig's parents was the worst. As we were talking of old houses, I thought of the last thatched house on the island, the one Dónal Doohan told me about, the one that was always full of smoke. 'Do you remember, Mary,' I asked, 'that thatched house at the east end where the two old sisters lived?'

Oh, I know. Gráinne and Nellie. Aye, the thatched house over there. I was there one night, myself and

Gráinne Duggan, and there was two boys along with us. We hadn't much sense at the time.

We were looking at this thatched house and the smoke coming out the door. So we walked in anyhow, to the house, and the two, the *créatúr*s, was sitting at the fire; and the fire it was as high as that, an open fire, and there was three bags of turf on one fire, it was that big;

three bags of turf.

And there was a wee lamp, a Sacred Heart lamp, about this size, lit; that's all they had.

And the house was all dark. You had to try and walk, to make your way of it, that's the way it was, till you got to someplace. There wasn't chairs or nothing.

And she had a cow here, just down *in* the kitchen. And the *cow* was sick.

And their brother was drowned. Paidí, that's what you called him, and their sister, the both of them was drowned. The two sisters, *créatúr*s, was left in the house there by themselves.

But, I'll tell you this. When we went in it scared the life out of us.

The cow was sick down here and very sick indeed she was, and they [the sisters] up and down and up and down in the kitchen. And one, she sat down beside me. I was round about ten years that time, no sense or anything.

She says, 'For God's sake,' she says. 'Paidí,' — that's the man that was drowned, Mary, the two was drowned — 'for God's sake,' she says, 'Mary and Paidí, *help* us tonight to put the cow on her feet.'

She had grey hair, you know, and funny looking. They weren't from the Tory generation [family] at all.

But she started calling them. Oh, *a thaisce*, she had her hands up and the house was dark. The house was full of smoke, the smoke going out the door, this wee lamp on a stool. They hadn't even, the *créatúr*s, the table. There's no curtain in the window, and by Christ, we weren't long in one place.

And when me and Gráinne ran — you know where the house is — there's a big drain there. The both of us went down into the drain. We didn't see nothing!

But d'ye know long ago, well I heard many a time since that that was their nature, you know, calling ones that was dead. That generation, them people. If anything would happen, that they were calling them to *help* them. Sure, you know yourself what help they could get. Sure they couldn't get a help.

The whole land, away down to the shore, that's their land. Oh, they were very good workers.

Oh, the *créatúr*s, yes. They had cows and they had sheep. And they were digging turf and they were setting potatoes and setting corn. And they had big stacks of corn, the *both* of them. And turf, they had four or five stacks of turf. And potatoes and everything. And they had a donkey too. Oh, yes, they were very good workers. The *had* to do it.

They had to do it.

I remember them well! ■

Dan Rodgers
(b. 1910)

Dan Rodgers, at age seventy-eight, is a powerful-looking man still: six feet tall, broad-shouldered and weatherbeaten, his large hands showing the effects of years of work with salty fishing lines and nets, and with the worn-smooth handles of spades and pitchforks. His one weakness was his eyes, never strong as a young man and now giving him much trouble. Yet in spite of his poor eyesight he was, to quote Patsy, 'determined to earn his living by fishing. And did so. '

In 1944, at one of the times when fish and money were scarce, Dan went to work in Scotland, the first of a total of four trips. On his return to Tory after six months (a time limit that was a wartime regulation) he built the house in which he now lives, and he and his wife, Biddy Whoriskey, moved out of the family house to live on their own. A year later they adopted Patsy Dan. (Adoption, or fostering in earlier days, is not unusual on Tory.)

The house is just at the back of Dónal Doohan's at the beginning of the lane known as the Bog Road that leads to Greenport. The Tory houses of a hundred years ago were made of stone, mortared with sand and lime. Dan's, like all the newest ones built with the help of grants from the Congested Districts Board during a period that began in 1903, is made of cement blocks plastered over and whitewashed. The colour of the trim of doors and windows and the tops of the gate posts leading into the yard varies sometimes, but it is usually a cheerful red. It is a comfortable house, though not as large as some on the island. There are rooms at the front, the 'upper room', which is at the gable end of the house behind the chimney, and the 'lower room,' which is at the other end. One goes 'up the room' to the former, 'down the room' to the latter. To the rear there is a small bedroom and a 'back kitchen'; upstairs there is one room at the gable end.

Now that Dan and Biddy live alone, the 'upper room' is not used and the fireplace is closed up; but a touch of unexpected elegance is found there in the mantelpiece and surround of iron painted white, brought from Glasgow to Tory for 'Lloyd's house', the living quarters for the Lloyd's signal station, built near the lighthouse in the latter part of the nineteenth century. The fire in the lower room, however, is always glowing. Biddy, now in her eighties, is not well and stays in bed until the late afternoon. Then she sits by the hearth until nine or ten o'clock, the tongs always close to hand for her frequent rearrangement of the half burned sods. There is often a cat sitting with her, either on her lap or balancing precariously on its haunches on the arm of the chair, its front claws anchored to her apron, purring happily.

Most Tory houses have china ornaments on the mantelpiece, a Sacred Heart picture, a photograph of the pope, and an electric or battery-run clock on the wall; somewhere in the room there is also the now ubiquitous television set. Dan and Biddy's house is no exception, but there is one pleasing difference: on a shelf above Biddy's chair is a handsome and dignified eight-day wind-up clock. It is framed in dark oak and below the face there is a design on glass of a large peacock, two smaller birds of unknown breed, an island with two trees on it and a schooner at anchor near by. A beaming sun shines over all. Through the design the brass pendulum can be seen swinging slowly to the slow rhythm of a firm tick-tock. The clock face is somewhat misted over — a combination of age and forty years of turf smoke — so that, although it is still possible to see the hands clearly, one cannot read the name of the maker or the date. Dan bought it in a second-hand shop in Glasgow in 1944 for twelve shillings and says that it was made in America in 1844. 'Think now,' he tells me proudly, 'all the way from the States to Glasgow and then to Tory.'

It was while sitting in Biddy's chair under the clock in the early afternoons, hearing the companionable ticking during the pauses in our conversations, that I taped Dan's stories. Dan was the first one I had asked to tell me about life on the island in his young days and I found it a delightful experience.

> Well, to tell you the truth now,
> all I can remember when I was growing up,
> d'ye see,
> this island.
> There was no dole, no pension. There were only yawls. All *fishing*.
> *Plenty* of fish and plenty of potatoes. But no *more*, no more. D'ye see.
> When I was going to school, not *me alone*, d'ye see, but the whole of the island, we would have to stay in bed in the morning, till the mother gets up and peel a pot of potatoes for us.
> And 'beetle' them, mashing them in the *pot*, d'ye see. And putting them on the plates.
> And we would sit around the table, we were six of a family there. And we had plenty of milk, plenty of potatoes. Plenty of *fish*.
> But no dole, no pension, hardly no flour at all, d'ye see.
> And no *shoes*, no boots, no anything.
> Maybe I was thirteen or fourteen years of age before I put on the first pair of *shoes*. And I'm telling you the God's *truth*. Not me alone as I said before.
> We go to school; and we have, that time, to carry a sod of turf, d'ye see. Under our arm to the schoolhouse.
> And the schoolmaster then would put down a fire — there was no word of heat, heaters. Nothing in the world like that d'ye see.
> And then at twelve noontime he would let us go then; we had nothing but to sit around the table much the same *again*.
> We would come back [from school] then at four o'clock.
> Maybe we would have a cup of tea *after*, d'ye see.

After school, well, I would go around the houses. They have a big habit of playing *cards*.

There was plenty of meat then.

You will see a man killing a cow or a beast of a bullock or something the day, d'ye see. And it was sure only four pence or six pence a pound,

that was all.

And then you'll see them around the table. And they would put out so many pounds of meat, d'ye see. And every person would stake six pence, or ten pence d'ye see, or the like of that, that would *cover* the four pound of meat that was out on the table, d'ye see.

And whoever get the biggest, *highest* number, d'ye see, he will be the winner, d'ye see. And when them eight would get up from the table, another eight would go on, ye see, and pay some money.

That's the way they were carrying on,

during the *winter time.*

You would see there was three or four, maybe four or five bullocks killed during the winter.

But I tell you the difference now and the change in this island.

Near all they have a horse and two cows, since I remember. And every house on the island has got a horse and a cow, at least.

So — they done away with *that*. The money got too plentiful. They've got too much money now.

They do away with the cattle, they do away with the hens, doing away with the *land*. They hardly set any potatoes now at all.

And I'm sure only for the tractors — they were damn lucky that the tractors come into the island — if it wasn't for the tractors, they would hardly set anything at all.

* * *

'When I was growing up, the women was doing far more than the men was doing at that time. Ye know.' Dan knew of what he spoke, for his mother had been widowed when the children were young and her life had been hard, as indeed it was for all women on Tory, whether widowed or married. Dan described the work they had to do on the land in addition to the regular household chores.

> There was a horse in every house and there was a fisherman, two fishermen in every house. That time they used to be fishing herrings around the cliffs.
>
> And instead of carts it was creels they have on the horses, d'ye know.
>
> And you would see the women, they would take the horse into the midden [dunghill near dwelling] and take a *graip* [manure fork] and fill the two creels.
>
> Just alone, a woman alone, ye know.
>
> And they would go about a quarter of a mile at least with that creel full of manure, spreading it on the potatoes. Back again then and into the same spot.
>
> And then when it's around twelve o'clock at day time, well they have to go to the cliffs with their husband's or their brother's dinner.
>
> So they would go in then, you know yourself, as far as Portadoon, or if the boat is not there maybe it landed over in Greenport,
>
> a long walk, d'ye know.
>
> And then they [the fishermen] would come in to the rock and put out an anchor, and [go] up on the hill. And then they would all sit about around and they would take their dinner, and then into the boat again.
>
> And down with the women then to start the whole job again, d'ye know.
>
> And if there was some corn to set or potatoes to manure, they would manure the potatoes.
>
> Maybe the husband or the brother would have a chance to come and cover the potatoes and plough the land, d'ye know.
>
> 'Set the corn for me and I'll take the horse and harrow it back again.'
>
> The women would harrow it back.

And then after May time there would be a lot of seaweed coming in ashore.

They would put on a big apron of bags.

They would cut a bag and make an apron of the bag and put it around their waist. Go down to the pier and then with a *graip* and they will fill them big creels with seaweed and walk about a quarter of a mile with that creel.

Then they would spend the half of the day putting out the seaweed.

Come in then, and feed the horse, make ready the dinner and eat the dinner, out then and take the *graip* and spread that seaweed under the sun.

And next day they come, that seaweed will be dry and then they will make what we call wee cocks of it, rickles;

we call that in Irish *gragán*.

And then when it was dry enough, they would take maybe four or five or six or seven of each rickle and make it into one.

And then you would see the women, when they have the potato crop finished, they would take a spade. And they would go up cutting turf — 'twas only sand, it wasn't up to much — what we call *scraith* [chippings of turf].

And then they would come then and make *gragán*s, as I told you before, of the turf.

And then when the *gragán*s would be dry enough, they would make big sacks of it.

They would take the horses and creels again — you would see them filling the creels — and drive them out a quarter of a mile to the man that was building the stacks of them for the winter.

Ah, they were working hard that time.

* * *

Dan Rodgers' father, Denis, was both fisherman and farmer, as was almost every man on Tory in those days. He and his wife Bridget, who came from Inishbofin Island, had six children, four boys and two girls. Denis died suddenly when Dan was only five years old. 'Died of appendix; give us our breakfast in the morning and dead that night,' Dan explained. The eldest child, William, was twelve, the youngest, Mary (McClafferty) was not quite two. Bridget's brother arrived from Inishbofin to help her, bringing with him a cow for extra milk for the children, but he could stay for only a short time. When he left, Bridget's brother-in-law, John Liam Feidhlimí Rodgers, came to live with her to help on the land and to add his earnings to what little she had.

John was much older than his brother Denis and had no family of his own, both his wife and his only child having died young. He was an educated man for he had gone on from the Tory primary school to two years of 'college' (secondary school) in Dunfanaghy; so in addition to being a fisherman he had another job, that of registrar of births, marriages and deaths on Tory. Every three months he would take his reports to the Labour Exchange in Dunfanaghy, walking there from the pier at Magheraroarty, a distance of ten or twelve miles. All the money he earned from fishing and as registrar and later from his old age pension, he gave to Bridget.

The registrar's books were kept in his house in a large box made of metal, in case of fire; but John had many story-books as well (as opposed to novels, which were considered sinful) and was an avid reader until, when quite old, he became blind. Dónal Doohan says that 'John knew the history and all about Tory,' and Dan and William quoted him when they told me their stories. After he died Bridget cleared out the books and gave most of them to other island families. They were eventually burned for, as Gráinne Doohan told me, 'They were lying around the houses and the old women used the pages to light their fires.' Dan and his brothers helped on the land and, as they grew older, fished. His sisters helped with the household chores, after school, and took care of the horse and cows. But in spite of their uncle's assistance, times were difficult and the children, like many others on Tory in those years, grew up aware only that life and hard work were inseparable.

* * *

Alfred McFarland noted that the islanders were

> ... mostly employed in field labour, or fishing, cutting wrack or making kelp: but fishing is the favourite pursuit, and turbot and cod, ling, haddock and plaice, braisers, herrings and gurnet, eels and breyans, gray-lords, lobsters and crabs, are caught in great abundance. Mackerel are also taken — as well as sprats; and occasionally the latter are so numerous, that they can be drawn up in hundreds, by creels let down from the cliffs. The islanders fish from a c*orragh* [currach]. The fishing is chiefly managed with rods and hand lines; as the islanders have neither nets, nor long lines, and the common limpet affords the principal bait.

Fishing, beef and fishing, meat and *potatoes*, that was all.

That was all at my time when I was growing up, and *before* that. Before that, now.

But then what I seen when I was growing up, of my father and my uncle and everybody on the island, ye see, every house on the island had a *currach*.

Well the job they have, they would dig limpets, ye know, them that grows on the rocks. And put them in *boxes*.

And they would take them over to the wife. And she would put the pot on the fire, and put the water boiling, and throw the limpets into the pot.

And then get them back again and take them out of the shell, and *then* put them into *these* boxes, for the husband or for the brothers.

Two [men] in each currach.

They would go out to Camas Mór — see where them buoys are anchored — out at the head of the pier.

They would go out there and they have a rope around a stone, and they would leave the stone go, and that stone would keep the currach in anchor,

while they would be there, d'ye see.

There were two in every currach and each man has a

fishing rod. Just made of wood. *Hand-made.* And a line and a hook.

And they will chew the limpets, and then they will take the limpets out of their mouth and put them on the hook and throw them out.

And as soon as they strike the sea at all, the fish would come and catch them.

And I can remember us coming in with from ten dozen to thirty dozen to forty dozen, every time we'd be *there.*

And then we would gut them. And wash them. And take them into the curing station [on Tory]. And selling them for five pence to six pence or seven pence or eight pence a dozen.

* * *

When a doctor was needed, a boat would have to go out to the mainland to get him and then take him back. William Harkin in 1893, TH Mason in 1936, and other writers, I'm sure, tell the story of the doctor and the Tory islanders; it may vary in length and manner of description, but the moral remains the same: greed does not pay. Hugh Curran of Gortahork told it to me as follows: 'A doctor was going in to Tory, you see, and he wouldn't go in unless he got his first fee. And the fee — I forget now what was the fee — I know he charged us two pounds one time; an awful fee it was, a man's wages that time was only about eighteen shillings a week, so he was asking for two weeks' wages. Well anyway, he went in; they gave him the money and took him in. But whatever the person would take him out, they wouldn't take him out until they doubled the fee. It was ten pounds for taking him out!' Dan remembers:

Even there was no *nurse* on the island. And there was no *doctor* on the island. At the time, when I was growing up.

And for instance now, if a person gets sick. Or a woman gets sick on the island. She needs a doctor.

We would have to go down to the pier there and pull

down a *boat*. We'd only a *yawl*, 'twas a sailing boat, d'ye see.

We would have to *sail* or to pull, out as far as Magheraroarty.

We would have to send for the *doctor*, whatever time till sunsets will come.

And take him to the patient. And examine the patient. Whether he is to hospital taken or not. Take the doctor back home again,

and come back to the island *that night again*.

I done that myself. I done that myself.

Well, it would take us two hours at least. And especially if the wind would be against you, ye see, it take you more than that.

And then during the winter time the herrings was very plentiful, but still and all the price wasn't too good.

I spent several years down in Downings. I spent four or five years, or maybe six or seven years up in Magheraroarty fishing. With a yawl.

I was over in Kincasslagh, I was over in Arranmore fishing herring, d'ye see, in the *winter* time, with yawls.

It was necessary to go out, d'ye see. And maybe the price wasn't so good.

And that time when *I* was growing up, there's another habit they have.

There was five boats in the east end with ring nets, and there was five ring nets in the west end. D'ye see.

And at May time, they was sure that they would have plenty of herrings. The trawlers weren't very plentiful at the time, d'ye see.

And they [the islanders] would *all* go to sea, d'ye see, and they would ring the herrings up just below the cliffs there. You would *see* the herrings bubbling in every direction.

And they have tenders — that's a *bigger* size of yawl — they would come down to the pier and pull them down, two in each boat, and they would row around as far as the net, where they have the herrings caught.

And then they would fill *that* yawl. And if that yawl wouldn't hold the herrings for them, they have to send for another one. And *then two in each boat* put out two big oars then, there on the north side. And pull up as far as Downings pier.

Eighteen miles.

And pull up as far as Bunbeg, up to *Kincasslagh*, with a cargo of herrings.

Maybe after landing *there*, maybe the curer will come down and make us throw them out. There's no price for them.

Oh, hundreds of times that's happened.

Well, I'm telling you.

Walk around there at the pier, start with the basket and the scoop — and *empty* the boat again on the way home.

Tory is in the track of the north Atlantic shipping and from the days of the first sailing ships there have been wrecks along its coast. But with the establishment of a Marconi direction-finding station near the lighthouse in the early 1930s the number was greatly reduced, and since the end of World War II, few, if any, ships have been lost.

In the old days, however, the salvage from the wrecks was of great benefit to the islanders. Wood, on a treeless island, had many uses; iron was employed in the making of the then somewhat primitive farming implements. I have seen the use of the old iron in hearths, as small foot-bridges over drains; and the long discarded 'home-made harrow whose teeth were ships' bolts' described by TH Mason is probably the same one that I saw lying for several years by the side of the road, across from Eilish and Éamonn Rodgers' house.

The flotsam and jetsam were spotted by the 'watermen', islanders whose volunteer job it was to walk around the shore, morning and evening, and look for anything that might have been washed up on the beach. This was a tradition of many, many years and continues to this day. As Patsy Dan told me, 'Those type of men called watermen was very valuable to the island indeed. Because if there was any type of boat in trouble, early in the morning or late in the evening, one would be sure that one of those would be around the shore, around the island, and they would be the first that would get the community on the alert, or will be telling the community of any such strange things happening.' Dan said:

> I remembered one night here, we were in the very need of something to eat. Well.
>
> A cargo of flour came over. From the east. A *ship* with a cargo of flour on it. You call the *Wheatplain*, ha, ha, ha!
>
> And out just about a hundred yards this side of Portadoon she just *ran* upside, much the same as she would run up beside the pier.
>
> You have only just to walk into her and put the bag of flour on your back. [Dan laughed delightedly.]
>
> She was grounded.
>
> The *skipper* was supposed to say this: that when he was about a quarter of mile off Tory, d'ye see, that a *man* come alongside him, and in the wheelhouse. And he took the wheel out of his hands.
>
> And that's how she landed.
>
> And then at low-water time, we took the punts and yawls down at the pier and rowed them alongside her, I had done it myself, myself and another two.
>
> There was a man down at the hatch and he was throwing up two-hundred-weight of bags, not a hundred-weight bags, but *two*-hundred-weight of bags.
>
> And I would carry them between my two hands, like this, and I would let them down to the two in the boat.

* * *

John O'Donovan wrote from Falcarragh on 15 September, 1935: 'I have given up the idea of landing on Tory for many reasons, among the strongest of which is that I might, in this stormy season, be detained a month upon it without being able to get back to the Continent of Tir-Connell [Co Donegal].' However, it seems that he had been able to talk with some of the islanders and was apparently pleased with the information he had been given about the island's antiquities. He was told about the 'Doon of Balor', Tor Mór, the 'Bed of Dermot and Gráinne', Balor's castle and the church that was dedicated to St Colmcille. He was told also of 'The *Claightheach* or Belfry called round tower by foreigners, ie. those who have read books and are not natives of Tory.' His informant, Donnell McRory, said that (translated from Irish) 'Colmcille built this for a bell, and they say that it was a small bell in the top of it.'

Dan Rodgers disagrees with the local tradition that the bell tower was built by Colmcille. 'Colmcille has nothing to do with that tower at all,' he told me firmly, and when I asked him to explain his reply was, 'If you travel all round Ireland, especially on the west coast, you will see *them*. The Danes had them for kind of a watch house, watching the coast, d'ye see. Wherever you see any of them built, it's in the bay, *facing* out the bay. No. Colmcille had nothing to do with it all.'

Dan's theory was somewhat confused, for the round towers were built not *by* the Danes but to prevent the Danes, or Vikings, from stealing monastic treasures. The round tower on Tory — the only one in Co Donegal — was, most historians agree, erected about the time of Colmcille and close to the monastic settlement. It is fifty-one feet in height and fifty-one and a half feet in circumference. Its arched door is eight and a half feet above ground level. In the event of a Viking attack the monks, carrying their valuable manuscripts and silver with them, entered the tower by means of a ladder, which they then pulled up after them. It was impossible for the Vikings to break in the door with battering rams because of its height.

Dr Edward Maguire holds that the eminent antiquary Dr Petrie never believed in the possibility (suggested by some) that the round tower on Tory might have been Conán's. He was 'much happier in view of his cherished theory regarding the origins and purpose of the round towers in discovering that the uniform tradition among the people, the arched entrance and the tapering bee-hive top of the Clog-teach, all confirmed his long-contested verdict'.

Mgr James Stevens, also of the same opinion, included the following verse in his *Illustrated Handbook of South-Western Donegal*:

> *Here was placed the Holy Chalice that held the Sacred Wine,*
> *And the gold cross from the altar, the relics from the shrine,*
> *And the mitre shining brighter, with its diamond, than the east,*
> *And the crosier of the Pontiff, and the vestments of the priest.*

Dan strengthened this theory, at least as regards monastic treasures:

> Well, that's another story I'm going to tell you now. You can see *them* ruins, down at the tower there, did ye see that. Well, this is what my uncle told me about it.
>
> 'Dan,' says he, 'whoever,' says he, 'whoever child that would be born,' says he, 'would be brought into this island,' says he, 'and *blessed* and *baptised*.' Ye can see the basin down there *yet* [near the tower].
>
> 'And,' says he, 'the *priest* that would be ordained, he would be brought into this island,' says he, 'and be ordained in the same spot.'
>
> 'And,' says he, 'whoever student would come,' says he, 'he would bring a chalice of gold or silver, a candlestick of silver, or something of silver.' D'ye see.
>
> And they would leave them behind.
>
> And one night this man, he fancied these. And he took a currach. And he put them into the currach.
>
> And when he was going down the bay, the *bird* came. Supposed to be a *puffin*.
>
> And *lay* on the 'bird' [bow] of the currach.
>
> Says he with this man, says he, 'Ye'd better turn back,' says he, 'and leave that where you got it.'
>
> And he had done so.
>
> 'And,' says my uncle, 'from that day,' says he, 'to *this* day, *that part of the currach*,' says he, 'where the bird lay, is called the "bird" of the currach.'

* * *

Until 1985 when a licensed bar was added to the community hall, there had not been a pub on Tory since Ward's public house was closed in the 1920s. During this dry period poteen was made by many families and, in later years, people would occasionally ask one of the lighthouse keepers to bring a bottle of whiskey back with him from the mainland when returning from shore leave. On a particularly chilly, damp day I arrived at Dan's house to discover that he had acquired an as yet unopened bottle, of excellent brandy, from which he poured me a generous helping in a wine glass. I took a few warming sips and then put it on the floor near the hearth, returning to it from time to time. It was a very generous helping indeed. 'Do tell me, today, about the cursing stone,' I asked Dan, settling comfortably in my chair with the tape recorder on my knee.

> I'll tell you about the cursing stone.
> For instance now, if you would wish to turn it on somebody, much of the same now if we go now and turn it on [Rev Ian] Paisley, ha, ha, ha, ha, ha!
> d'ye *see*.
> It was some kind of *possession*.
> And they were supposed to turn her on the *Wasp*. That was a gunboat, a British gunboat. Ireland was under the British flag at the time. They were coming to transport the islanders. Well, it was *my* auntie, the last woman on the island that knew where that stone was. And d'ye know, she didn't let nobody know where it was because it would make more harm than good.
> If you and I would start fighting tonight,
> ha, ha, ha, ha,
> ahhh, the first thing tomorrow when I would get up, I would turn the stone on you, d'ye see!
> It might do more *harm* than *good. Ye know*!

There was a pause in the conversation and I sat silently for a while, once more aware of the soothing tick-tock of the clock on the shelf above my chair. Dan broke the silence. 'Finish up your drink, now,' he admonished me, 'it's not getting any stronger!'

* * *

Seán Ó hEochaidh told me a story of a man from Donegal, a non-Catholic, whose serious problem with rats in his haystacks was solved when he met a Tory man at a fair in Letterkenny and was told about the holy clay: 'I was actually talking to the man himself who *came* to Tory and who *got* the clay. And he shook it around the stacks. And he *swore* to me that it was a *fact* that the rats disappeared.' Dan has no doubts as to the abilities of the holy clay, and its remarkable power over rats and sea animals.

> Well. I'll give you an example now.
>
> I was over in Scotland during the war, d'ye see, I was working with a *farmer*. And this is a *true* story.
>
> And they were all Protestants, d'ye see.
>
> And I was stopping in what they called that time a *bóitheach* [bothy, hut], d'ye see.
>
> And the Irish people that were stopping in the *bóitheach* before we was in, the rats was picking the crumbs off the table. And *as soon as we arrive,*
>
> the rats disappear.
>
> Myself and another chap, God rest him he's dead now, and eight of a Land Army — that's girls, women working with the farmer.
>
> And the *grieve* was there, what we call the grieve, that's him that was the foreman. We call him the *báille,* in Irish, d'ye see.
>
> Says *he* — and the whole work crowd was around at the time — '*How* is it,' says he, 'that you boys,' says he, 'can chase these rats?'
>
> I was wondering how did he hear it.
>
> 'Who *told* you so?' says I.
>
> 'I *heard* it,' says he.
>
> 'Well,' says I, 'it's the holy clay of the island,' says I. 'We *always* carry it in our pockets. Especially,' says I, 'when we are at sea. It's the only thing,' says I, 'we depend on. And that if we go into any difficulties at all at

sea,' says I, 'we take out this holy clay,' says I, 'and bless it in the name of the saint, ye see.' And so.

'Would *that* clay's up there,' says he, 'would it do the same?'

'And it would,' says I. 'There would be no rats there.' D'ye see.

'Do you not give in?' says I, for he didn't say whether he did or not, d'ye see.

I says, 'Go now,' says I, 'and get a rat for *me*. Not a dead one,' says I.

'And *I'll* make a ring there with the holy clay now,' says I, 'and I'll *bet* you a pound,' says I, 'she'll die in the ring before she goes across it.'

'Heh, heh, heh,' that's the answer I got.

And I just went out to the hill with one of the workers. Says *he* to me — he was a Protestant too — '*You*,' says he, 'have some religion,' says he, 'but we have none.'

'Well,' says I, 'I'm coming from the west. And that's our religion.'

And that's about the holy clay now.

Dan spoke of using the holy clay 'Especially when we are at sea.' Seán Ó hEochaidh had told me: 'I'd say not alone that *Tory* people carried it in their boats; but along the coast right up from Malin Head to Teelin Head, every fisherman got a grain of that clay. They all had it in their boats. There were two things that they generally had in the bow of the boat: one was a very small bottle of holy water and the other was the holy clay.' Patsy Dan, Dan's son, described the use of the clay from personal experience.

> This was the belief of every islander and the community, and still is. If a sea animal happened to come across in front of your boat, you would be very, very much afraid that you mightn't see home ever again, because there could be an awful threat by a sea animal — big or small the boat may be — a currach above all or a small punt.

I went through this myself once, I remember, with my father about fifteen or twenty years ago. And one of us went up to the bird of the currach; it was a currach that we were oaring at the time, and many years ago. And we took the little bag down and we took out a pinch of the holy clay and we blessed ourselves, and my father took off his cap. And we asked that, through the power of the saint that was buried along with the *mórsheisear*, the clay would protect us against the sea animals or any other difficulties. And we said a Hail Mary and another prayer to Our Lord — just one or two short prayers — and then we sprinkled out the holy clay onto the sea. And by that the sea animal vanished away.

So I saw that, as a matter of fact, happening myself, but it was just once and that was enough for me. But in the old days many of the old people have seen this happening and they have worked with the clay over and over again. Because in those days, with a lot of herrings around the island, there would be a lot of whales and sharks and every sea animal like that around the island. And the fishermen could hardly go a number of hundred yards away until they would meet with one of those sea animals at all times.

So this is why that holy clay was very important indeed, and this is why it was in every punt and every boat and in every currach, up to this day as well.

* * *

Here's another story I'm going to tell you now.

There was several boats in the east end and there was several boats in the west end, d'ye see, *fishing* boats.

And *each* boat would have to make a turn to go out to the mainland with the priest. There was no engines at the time, no motor boats at the time, and I have done it myself.

I remember going out — not me alone but a crew of the boat went out to Magheraroarty one day with a priest.

And he was a *Scotchman*, he was just here on holidays.

'Well,' says he, when we landed in Magheraroarty, says he, 'I'm very sorry,' says he, 'I have no money to give you.'

'Well,' says we, 'we are not *expecting* any money from you.'

'But,' says he, 'I'll give you things,' says he, 'far *better* than money.'

He put us all into the boat. And he bless ourselves and he bless the boat. And he give us what *we* call a Sacred Heart, *each* of us.

'As *long* as you can carry this in your pocket,' he says, 'or anywhere, your mouth,' says he, 'is never going to touch water.'

You couldn't get any money better than *that*. And that was all right, we were very happy with that.

And *this* is the most wonderful thing that ever happened to me or to any other body.

I folded it up in a wee piece of a cloth, along with some other things, d'ye see. And I always used to carry it in my pocket.

And that time at the *harvest*, we would go out to Magheraroarty, along with the Magheraroarty people, along with the Inishbofin people, fishing *herrings*, day and night.

And, I was stopping in a house over in Curransport and I forgot *this* [medal] and I was *very sorry*, when I haven't it.

And *this* day, at dinner time, I was sitting at the table, eating a potato. I was having a chat with the family of the house. I was sitting on a stool. When I feel this, under my bum. *Bothering* me, d'ye see.

Much the same now as if I was sitting on a *pocket* knife or a pipe, or the like of that.

I just put down my hand between my trousers and the stool, and I pull it up.

What have I?

but what I was looking for!

I'm wondering, *from that day to this day*, who left it there and where did he come?

'Twas a *miracle*.

Dan had no sooner finished his story than he suddenly leaped to his feet, grabbed a broom and with loud *shoo*ing noises and mutterings of 'lucky black cat', chased the intruder — which must have come in through the back kitchen window — out the front door. It seemed an opportune moment for me to leave with a promise to return the next day.

The next afternoon, after we had settled beside the fire, I mentioned the cat. 'Yesterday when we were talking and the black cat came running through the room, you said, "That's a *lucky* black cat."'

'Well, it was.'

'In the United States, black cats are usually considered *unlucky*. What would you consider an unlucky sign on Tory?'

It did not surprise me that Dan, as a fisherman, believed that red was a bad omen. Anything red, even a fox glimpsed sitting on a cliff as one put out to sea, boded ill. To meet and particularly to be spoken to by a red-haired woman was a disaster.

'Well, that time, if a person, or a crew of a boat, would be going to fish, some of the women they would meet, they would rather turn back home.'

'Was it just because they had red hair?' I asked, 'or was there some other reason?'

'You'll meet a man in the morning, or a woman in the morning, they'll go beside you without speaking. You'll hardly know they were there now. Ye see. But you'll meet another [red-haired] woman and she'll say, "You're up very early this morning, it's a very good morning." Look at the difference between the two. The half of the fishermen would rather turn back home again.'

'Dónal told me,' I said, 'that it was not safe to walk between a ginger woman and the cliff. That she might "put you away". Was that true?'

Dan, who was not usually in accord with Dónal, nodded agreement. He continued then to talk about fishing.

They were always fishing, that time. *Fishing*, d'ye see.

But another habit they have that time, they would go up to the cliffs, and look east and west to see where they would see a ship coming back or forward.

They were all sailing ships at that time, and they were giving them a lot of grub. *Biscuits* and everything you want.

And *my uncle* got in a boat one day and he went to one of these ships. And the skipper asked him, 'Where are *you* from?'

'From Tory Island.'

And he says, 'Where does Tory Island lie? When *you* could put out to sea?'

The skipper didn't see the island, d'ye see.

And he gave them a cargo of stuff, bread and sugar, and they used to give them a lot of treacle for making poteen.

What came on them but *fog*. And they were out three days.

And my grandmother, she was the only one on the island, that has this prayer. If she would say this *prayer* three times, one after the other, *without a break*, it would be all right.

But that time there was a habit they have, they would have a *wake* in every house. They would start, put a table in the middle of the house with two candles, and a plate of tobacco. And they haven't got any wooden pipes, they have only *clay* pipes, d'ye see. And there was only four pence for half an ounce of a twist of tobacco that time.

And *my* uncle was there too [in the boat], and still and all my grandmother always said, '*They're alive wherever they are.*'

She would say this prayer. What we call it in Irish, that time, Liodán Mhuire [Litany of Mary], in *Irish*, d'ye see, but I couldn't tell you in English.

And every time she would say it, 'They're still alive,' she'd say. And still they were carrying on with the wake. A wake in each house. From morning till night.

But he *told* me, my uncle — God rest him now, he was in the boat — they landed, says he, in Greenport.

And the habit they have that time — and the Inishowen people out there they have it still — they would lift the oars *out*. It's oarlocks now they use, but it was two pins they have at that time.

And they would have the oar in between two pins. And then to make the boat light for them to haul up, they would lift the oar *out* of between these two pins and put them into the shore,

headwise.

And whoever would be on the beach they would catch the oars, headwise, and pull them up.

And [when the boat landed at Greenport] *each oar* went to bits. Each oar of the four oars, ye see, when this man got a hold of them and pulled them up, he says they went to bits.

He told me that. It's *no lie* that.

'But, Dan,' I asked, 'what made the oars go to bits?'

'It was a miracle that hit them.'

'The boat just came in on its own then? They weren't able to row?'

'They were starved with hunger. Three days out at sea with no food at all, d'ye see. They were perished.'

I was startled. 'They were perished? You mean they were dead?'

'No, no,' Dan answered patiently. 'They were living till old age after that. My uncle, he lived till he was eighty-eight.'

I learned later that by the word 'perished', Dan had meant that they had been very cold.

* * *

On another afternoon Dan told me a little more about the way in which families lived in the days of the thatched houses: the days before the Congested Districts Board bought Tory from the Manchester businessman Joule in 1903 and, with grants, built houses, the slipways and the pier, helping the islanders earn a more profitable living. The Congested Districts Board was, to quote Robin Fox, 'That exemplary body founded on funds from the disestablished Irish church by Balfour in his attempt to "kill home rule with kindness". '

> Centuries ago there was no slates on the roofs, d'ye see, they were all thatched houses. And you would wonder the way they would have them nice and tidy.
>
> But the most wonderful thing I'm wondering about when they would get married.
>
> One of them would take in the wife, or the wife would take in the man; and maybe there was six or seven of a family there before them.
>
> Many's a time I'm wondering how *well* they put up with one another, d'ye see.
>
> And the most wonderful thing in the world. *Down* there at the other end of the house, that's where they would have the cattle in. And the horses.
>
> You would see a cow — I didn't see much of that but I was told — or maybe two cows, in this side of the house. And the other side of the house you would see a horse.
>
> And when the horse would see you moving about through the house, you will see him *stamping* his feet, like this. '*Give* me something to eat,' ha, ha, ha, ha, ha!
>
> And then the cow. If the cow would see them going about the house, the cow would start it. 'Give me some potatoes,' or 'Give me something to *eat*.'
>
> And there was a cradle beside the fire at the same time. There was maybe a child in the cradle. And maybe the child would start to cry.
>
> Ha, ha, ha, ha! *I'm telling you* there was some carrying on.
>
> And another thing, they would have a big family that time, as I was told by one of the old men. Maybe up to thirteen there in every family.
>
> And they weren't able to build a house, d'ye see. They haven't got the monies to build a house. They would mostly all live together.

And the most wonderful thing I was wondering about, how *well* they put up with one another.

But thank God I didn't see the like. The island improved that much since I remember. And then the government looked after them.

The first thing they do, they give them a grant to build a house for themselves.

And they did away with the thatched. And put on the slates.

That's one thing good the government have done for them.

One thing good.

* * *

Although poteen was nearly always available on Tory, any liquor of known, or unknown, source was much appreciated. Patsy Dan told me that up until the 1950s, small French trawlers fished for lobsters near the rocky coast. The islanders gave the crews fresh eggs, and, in return, were given wine. According to Patsy, the French were particularly adept at throwing a coiled rope from the trawler to the shore. When the islanders caught it, the crew would tie a wine bottle to their end of the rope and the men on shore would haul it in. This was the known source.

The unknown source had, sometimes, unexpected results. One day Kathleen Rodgers' father's cousin, Hudai Whoriskey, found a large barrel washed up on the beach. It had 'France' written on it and other words that he could not make out. The liquid it contained had little or no odour. While Hudai was thinking about what to do with this treasure trove, along came a friend and the two discussed the situation. Kathleen told me, 'And this fellow says, "I'll bet you five pounds will you take a sip of it." "Well," says my uncle, "I'll take a sip off the barrel," he says, "but I'll make the will first." He said, "I want to lie beside my mother over in the old graveyard, and my father to look after the donkey and the horse." So he took anyway the full glass of it, and collapsed. So anyway, they took him in — he was living on his own — and they had him lying on the floor, and every five minutes they would go in and see how he was doing. He was still lying there. This was about twelve o'clock at night. And about five o'clock in the morning they went in, and sure he was singing, sitting singing, on his arse, on the floor! So then they all took sips of the moonshine... '

Dan was kind enough to give me his own recipe for making poteen. It was in great detail and so, unfortunately, or perhaps fortunately, too long to include here. I learned one thing, however, that when the brew is 'doubled' [put twice through the still] it is very strong. Dan gave me a good example; 'I remember myself here when we have the tilly [lamp] instead of the electric. You had to light it with methylated spirit, stick a tort [wick] into the methylated spirit and give it a match. But I was lighting the tilly with the *poteen*.'

Madge Rodgers
(1898–1986)

Although Madge Rodgers, as she grew old, spent the winter months in Falcarragh on the mainland with Peggy and Ruairí Rodgers, she lived on Tory with another son and daughter-in-law for the rest of the year. She always said, as did others of her generation, that she felt better when she was on the island. She was in her eighties when I used to go to see her in Seán and Maureen's comfortable house on the far side of West Town. By early afternoon she was downstairs, sitting in her special corner of the settee by the fire, her grey hair in neat plaits, a colourful shawl around her shoulders, and usually two or three sleek, tiger-striped cats curled companionably near her feet. She enjoyed her grandchildren, liked the conversation of neighbours and of visitors who came, as I did, from far away, and was looked after by her daughters-in-law with consideration and affection.

Like many of the women her age, Madge was modest about her ability to speak English; she spoke it well but she was shy about doing so. One afternoon I asked if she would tell me of just one thing that happened when she was a child, something that she remembered in particular. In her gentle, low voice she told me of the wreck of the liner *California*, a merchant ship of the Anchor Line that ran ashore off the lighthouse in thick fog in June, 1914.

> When I was a wee girl, the most exciting thing I had was one night of a heavy *fog*, and the big liner *California* was wrecked on the island.
> And we were up, as wee girls we were up where the

hall is now. We had a plank there and we had a few barrels and we were paying see-saw.

And three or four of my own age, girls, were playing see-saw there when we heard the noise; we heard the siren blowing and shots sprang up in the air,
and we knew something was up.

So we ran down to our house, it was the nearest house here now, we ran down and I called my mother. She was in and she was standing at the table doing something. And I asked her where my father was and she says that my father was down putting in the *cows*.

So I ran down to the byre, where at the tower he had the byre that time, and I told him about what we heard,
something *strange*.

And my father said he heard that himself too, and he tied up the cows, he came up and ran over to where the ship was, and then we *all* went over. *Every one of us* and my mother and all,
everyone on the island went to see the sight.

And they were firing breeches buoys or something to the shore. It was full of people, you know, the liner, *all* full of people, poor *créatúr*s.

They phoned away for two ships and two other big ships came to their assistance, the *Ranger* and the *Linnet*, that was their names.

I remember that well. We used to be over there.

And they took all the passengers away. And I heard that there was a young baby born on the way from America, on the ship.

And they were all taken away safe, thank God, taken away safe from the ship, from the *California*.

She ran ashore in heavy fog, it was very thick. This side of the lighthouse. Aye, I think it was a kind of flatty place where they landed; that's where she was calmed, like.

And then they took all the passengers away the following day. We'd seen them picking them down. We were over, we were over nearly all night. We had little sleep, *watching*.

* * *

In the gale in which Dónal Doohan's grandfather, Roger Doohan, was lost, Madge's grandfather, Paidí Heggarty, was among the six others who also lost their lives. Her son Seán told me that on the day of the storm twenty currachs were out fishing about a mile off the lighthouse. When the northerly wind began to blow, some of the men stopped fishing and were able to reach the safety of Port an Churraigh [Port of the Currach], a sandy strand just to the east of the present pier, a place where the light currachs could be beached easily. The others continued to fish a little longer, hoping that with the wind at their back they could paddle, if need be, to the mainland without too much difficulty. The wind became a gale. It carried the currachs to the shore, nine miles away, where they were dashed against the rocks. Paidí Heggarty managed to get a footing on a rock below the village of Meenacladagh and called for help, but although he was seen and his cries were heard, no one came to his rescue. Seán said that the mainland people fished but 'they were not islanders, they were not so used to the sea'. They were, like many other fishermen along the coast, deeply superstitious about saving a drowning man. So Paidí Heggarty was left on the rock until, exhausted, he slipped into the water. When the body was washed ashore, it was carried up from the beach but it was not taken into a house. 'They left him in the garden [any small place enclosed by a wall] until the family could go out and bring him back to Tory,' said Seán. There were seven new widows on the island that night.

> There was only my father in the family, my *father* was the only one my grandmother had.
>
> And *he* was only eleven years, he's told me many's a time, he was only eleven years when his father was drowned. He told me that many a time, because that was long before *my* time.
>
> His sister went out and she brought in his corpse, aye,

and he's buried down in that graveyard. That's what I heard.

He said it was *Palm Sunday*. He never liked *Palm* Sunday after that, he never cared for Palm Sunday. And I often ask him *why*. He says, 'That was the day,' he says, 'my father's corpse came in to die. *That's why.*'

It was a sad day for him. Aye.

And there were two in each currach. A gale came on them, you know, and they went as far outside as they [thought they] could be safe. If they could *swim,* but they weren't able to swim.

My grandfather, he went up on a rock, and he was on the rock and he was calling out for help to the people across the way. They never heed; they never bothered about him.

And he was calling till the sea washed him down again from the rock. That's how he was drowned.

And then when he was washed out ashore, his corpse was brought up somewhere. But no house would let him in, his corpse. Aye. They had a wish that time about that. They thought if they were to let in a corpse that someone else in the house would be drowned.

Aye, that was it. Aye, I heard that again. Aye.

And his sister went out and brought him in, and buried him in the graveyard. That's what I remember. It was long before my time, but I heard my father telling me.

He never liked the people outside since, in Meenacladagh they call it. He never cared for them. They're a bad crowd.

Pádraig Óg Rodgers
(1904–1988)

In 1982, the year following my very brief afternoon trip to Tory, I spent almost three weeks in the island. During this time I met, among others, Pádraig Óg Rodgers, 'king' of Tory, and his sister Annie. Annie had been ill for some months so that on my visits I saw her only briefly and my conversations were mostly with Pádraig. I went out to the mainland for five or six days and on my return I heard that Annie was failing fast; she died a short time later.

When it was evident that Annie had but little time left, the island priest ordered a coffin to be put on board the trawler so that it could be brought in as soon as it was needed, although in spite of this forethought its arrival was delayed for two or three days due to stormy weather. Patsy Dan told me that in the old days, when mainland coffins were not affordable, when transporting anything quickly from the mainland was a doubtful possibility, the coffins were made on the island. Any available bits and pieces of wood, from flooring to timber left over from boat building, were utilised. They were then 'varnished' with a chocolate brown dye made from bark, which was used, 'going way back in time', for colouring and preserving the sails of the fishing boats.

In the *Dictionary of Mythology, Folklore and Symbols* (New York, 1962), keening is described as 'An Irish lament for the dead. Said to have been invented by St Brigid. Always sung by women, frequently professional mourners. An expression of grief, which originally may have been intended as a howl to call the soul back from the dead.' Edmund Spenser (1552–99), who believed that the ancient, pre-Christian Nemedians came to Ireland from

Scythia, wrote in *View of the State of Ireland*, 'There be other cryes also used among the Irish, which savour greatly of the Scythian barbarisme, as their lamentations at the buryals, with despairfull out-cryes and immoderate waylings... '

I went to Annie's wake with Patsy Dan. I was new to Tory and its ways and so, feeling a stranger, I stayed only long enough to sit for a few minutes in the room where Annie was laid out, and to pay my respects to Pádraig Óg. Wakes have changed a little over the years: the clocks are no longer stopped at the hour of death; cigarettes take the place of clay pipes; and music may be played in the house before the end of a full year. And no longer is there any keening, that wild, heartfelt outpouring of grief as the coffin leaves the house on its way to the church and, later, on its arrival at the graveyard. Annie herself was the last person on Tory to keen. Mary McClafferty, a 'terrible' keener in her own right, told me: 'That was the last crying on Tory Island. Annie Rodgers. That's round about seven years ago now, when Jimmy [her brother] died. She, *créatúr*, was standing at the door when the coffin came down, and she was crying 'Jimmy, Jimmy' and she had her hands clapping. Everybody was crying, looking at her. And she was *crying* the *whole way* [to the church]. Till we went in to the chapel we hear the sound. But there's no crying since.'

Still, much of the old tradition still remains. No work, except for the most essential, is done from the time of death until after the funeral. Friends, often chosen ahead of time, come to help with the laying out of the body; they come to make tea and to prepare food at stated intervals during the length of the wake, usually two days; and always there are no less than two people sitting continuously in the house, helping to comfort the bereaved with the warmth of their presence, and to pass the hours with conversation. And in each of the two rooms used, there is still 'the wee square table with a white cloth on it' upon which there are two candles on either side of a small crucifix, a bowl of holy water, and two plates, one containing tobacco, the other snuff.

Six years after Annie's funeral, I was on Tory when another death occurred. Mary Hughie Rodgers, a lively, cheerful woman who had been in the hospital on the mainland for several months after suffering a severe stroke, came back to the island. The Commissioners of Irish Lights helicopter, on its bi-monthly run with the doctor, brought her in in the morning. She was taken in a wheelchair to her house, facing the bay, and died ten minutes later by the fire while her family was making her a cup of tea. It was a great shock to everyone; but at least Mary Hughie was back home on Tory and by her own hearth, as she had wished. This time when I went to the wake I stayed, as custom dictates, for at least an hour, sitting chatting or in silence; now among friends, no longer feeling like a 'foreigner'. During one of the silent moments, I suddenly thought how strangely coincidental it was that, as I heard the roar of the helicopter, landing on the grass in front of the Red House across the road from Eilish's, bringing Mary back, I had just begun to transcribe the tape which follows, a description of wakes on Tory in the old days as Patsy Dan remembered them.

> When the news would get out on the island that somebody had died, the people would wait until the body was laid out; and then, in a matter of three to four hours, they would start going to the wake.
>
> As they would enter the house — if you were wearing a cap, you would take your cap off — they would say a prayer and go into the kitchen. Now, usually the body wouldn't be laid out in the kitchen, it would be either in the upper room or in the room down below. You would see a wee square table there, usually a wee square table, with a white cloth on and a small crucifixion and a candle lit on each side of the crucifixion. And a small holy water font there, right beside the crucifixion; and a small, old-style saucer with snuff on it, a wee lock of snuff on it, and another small saucer old-style, with a wee lock of tobacco on it.
>
> And then, let's say, that it was coming up to midnight. Then every one at the wake would be expecting the priest to come and he would appear around eleven thirty or about that. And would have a short conversation with the relatives of the deceased and then

would go to the room where the body was laid out. And then all the relatives that had been in the kitchen would move to the room. And many others too. And then five decades of the Rosary would be said and each of the relatives would say a decade of the Rosary. And all the decades that they were saying would be relayed up to the kitchen, and out to the corridor if anyone was there. So that everyone could hear what they were saying.

Most of the people would move then, after the priest would go — roughly ten minutes or a quarter of an hour after saying the Rosary — they would move from the kitchen down again to where the body was laid out. There would be the same in the room as there was in the kitchen; a small table, usually a wee square table, with a white cloth on and a crucifixion and a candle lit on each side, day and night, twenty-four hours around the clock. And, of course, there would be no time in the house at all, all clocks would be stopped when the person would die.

Then the people there would start chatting with the relatives, so as to take some of the worry off their mind. And talk about farming and talk about fishing and talk about very interesting news indeed. And all that they had to say would be discussed that night or during the day, at the wake.

Then that would go on for two nights and two days and then the third morning the funeral would take place. I remember also that the people would come in turns, to the wake, and stay for an hour, two hours and some of them even up to three hours. And then the worst time, the most lonely time, for the relatives would be around five to six o'clock in the morning, and coming well early in the morning.

But there was one in particular I remember, a man called John Diver, God rest him now, he died about a year ago at the age of ninety-three, and he will really be remembered for the tradition he was carrying out, as coming to almost *every* wake that was on this island during his lifetime, calling in to the wake at between five and six of the morning. Two mornings in a row. That would be the hardest time for the relatives; and especially the last morning, the funeral morning, because when the lid would go on the coffin, which would be roughly eight or nine in the morning, then the keening would start.

And he was one of those men who was really capable of standing out to this, when maybe a number of teenagers [who had come to make the tea] would leave the wake. They would leave because of the keening, oh indeed yes, indeed yes. But there was those of them that was able to stand it out, ye know, and could understand the grief and sorrow of the relatives.

And then the funeral would take place around eleven o'clock Mass. And if it was in the East Village that the wake was on, then in those days it would leave the East Village around an hour and a half or two hours before Mass. Because in those days it was a cart, a donkey and a cart, to bring over the coffin on. Now it's a tractor. But in the old days it was a cart, a donkey and a cart, and it would take some time, it would have to be limited to speed, so to say. And there would be bags of corn underneath the coffin, packed, bags of corn or hay so that the coffin wouldn't be getting bad bumping, ye know. And then they would reach the chapel, and the Mass then, and then they would go from the chapel to the graveyard. And that was the most [dis]heartening hour of the lot.

And then also, in those years, there was a man there that used to stand up before the funeral was over, or the body was buried, and would collect roughly half a crown, maybe more, from those who were able to afford it; but usually half a crown — and *less* too — to help the priest in his duties and to keep up the parochial house and the chapel; because there wasn't much other support going at the time.

And then when that was done and dealt with by this

special person, an old person, the keening then would start again. And they could be on there for an hour. And sometimes, even I saw myself, that they would have to be lifted by other relatives [from the grave] and then they would go down again, just clutched down again on their two knees, and start again. As it was quite scary, it would interfere with [upset] you a lot. And even I saw at funerals they being driven out by their relatives, because they could faint very easily. Not alone that it was a tradition, but they couldn't help it.

The keening? Oh my goodness, 'twas horrible for me anyway. And for many others, too. It would go on as an ordinary type of song. You would swear to yourself there was maybe ten verses in it, and it would continue on without a break. And whatever that person that died had been doing, if he was a farmer, [the song would tell] that he was a good worker, that he would come home, no matter where he would go after his day's farming and, ye know, this like. And if he was a fisherman, that many's the time he had fish, and come home, and many's a time he brought some money into the home and so on. All in the keening, oh dear aye. And they would clap their hands as well.

Well, there was of course again different women, there was special women that could cry and oh, you would prefer to be a thousand miles away. And there was others that could keen quite calm and low volume, so to say. My auntie [Mary McClafferty] she was quite strong and along with that she was a very good singer, I mean she had a brilliant voice, and that made all the difference too. Oh dear, she could really keen, yes, and her sister also, Una. Oh dear aye, yes.

* * *

In the summer of 1982, the summer of Annie's death, my knowledge of Tory and its people was limited to what I had learned from my correspondence with Patsy Dan. My conversations with Pádraig Óg Rodgers added to this germ of understanding. It was the beginning, as well, of a friendship that lasted until his death. His was the first house I visited on my arrival: 'Céad míle fáilte [A hundred thousand welcomes]' was his greeting. 'It's good to see you, Dorothy.' Then, with a smile and a little chuckle, 'The king welcomes you to Tory.'

Pádraig Óg Rodgers was a man of small stature but of great presence. Sitting in his chair by the fire, wearing his habitual turtleneck jersey and tweed cap set at a jaunty angle, he received his visitors with the dignity expected of 'royalty'. Many people came to see him and to listen to his fund of stories. His reading, too, was eclectic. When I was on Tory in August, 1988 (Pádraig had died in January of that year), his son and daughter-in-law invited me to look through his library and to choose a book from it as a remembrance. In the quite large collection there were many books on lighthouses and fishing boats, two of his major interests. There were books of Irish poetry, articles on Co Donegal, various dictionaries, several books on how to compose letters for all occasions, a large tome entitled *Universal Home Lawyer*, John Newman's *Apologia Pro Vita Sua* and, somewhat surprisingly, *The Way of the Sufi* by Idries Shah.

Pádraig had a wide circle of correspondence. He wrote in a flowing script and I was always pleased to find an envelope addressed to me in his elegant hand and to read the letter signed, 'I remain, as ever, your affectionate friend, Pádraig Óg'. He was proud of his calligraphy and, in particular, about the pen he used. Only a Waterman with a special nib would do; I sent him three pens before he found the one that suited him. He always returned a favour and in return for the pen, which I had insisted on giving him as a present, he gave me a photocopy of an extraordinary small pamphlet, *Tory Island Letters*. The only edition of this entertaining little work that Robin Fox could find is in the British Library of Political and Economic Science, London School of Economics.

Pádraig and I talked of a variety of things. Of one thing there was no doubt and that was his deep feeling for his island. A little of what he did for Tory is included in the following excerpts from his obituary notice in the *Donegal Democrat*, sent to me by his daughter Eilish:

> A day of mourning was observed on Tory Island on Sunday when the islanders came together to bid farewell to their elected 'King', Pádraig Óg MacRuairí... Pádraig was proclaimed as 'Rí Thoraigh' by popular vote of the islanders in 1940. He represented the interests of Tory, at home and abroad, from that time until his death last Friday evening, at the age of 84 years. During his lifetime he had occasion to correspond with leaders of Church and State. He fought for the rights of the islanders and made their case with the Donegal County Council, Health Board, Fisheries Board and various government Departments... There was an acute shortage of food on the island during the early thirties and Pádraig Óg was selected to go to Dublin to explain the position to Mr Eamonn De Valera who was President of the Executive Council at the time. He met Mr De Valera on 25th February, 1934... On the arrival to Tory Island on the 19th July, 1947, of Mr Eamonn De Valera, it was Pádraig Óg who delivered the official welcome speech... He took part in many programmes on Raidió na Gaeltachta, and he spoke in a deep lyrical voice... messages of sympathy were received from all parts of the country.

It was a week after Annie Rodgers' wake and funeral that I met Pádraig Óg's son, Paul, on his way to the post office and walked beside him for a few minutes. I asked him if he thought it might give his father pleasure if I were to stop by some afternoon and suggest that he tell me some stories, for I knew how much he enjoyed talking about the old days. Paul's reply, just before he pushed open the blue door of the post office, was 'There's nothing like good crack [interesting conversation] with a woman to make him feel better.' I went to see Pádraig the following day. I walked into the comfortable house, built many years ago by his father, and found the 'king' sitting by the fire. He was obviously affected by the death of his sister but seemed happy to have company. After a few words about Annie and a moment while we both looked into the glowing pattern made by the turf in the grate, I asked Pádraig if he had ever had any experiences with ghosts and fairies. I knew little about the habits of Irish ghosts and fairies. Thirteen summers and autumns spent in Invernessshire, however, from the age of eight to twenty-one, had well acquainted me with the Scottish variety and I had never had any difficulty in believing that such things might indeed exist. Tory, small and isolated, seemed an ideal place for these singular characters. I explained to Pádraig my interest and asked if he would be good enough to share some of his experiences with me. 'Well I will, surely, Dorothy,' he replied and, with scarcely a break, told me the following stories.

> Now.
> I quite remember my own cousin, she was only dead about three weeks.
> And I happened to just go to a certain house, to listen to the radio. And on the way, the wind was blowing from the south. And by the time I went down to this house, down to hear the radio news, the wind shifted *aird* [direction] to the north.
> I came back to the north side of my own home, and I knocked. And my sister answered me.
> 'Whoever you are,' she says, 'go back to the other door, the lee door. The wind has changed.'
> And on my way coming back just at the gateway between the gate and the garden, I saw the image of my own cousin, walking down the road. And the hand was going. And she was looking over on the opposite houses.
> And there was a big heap of ashes near by the road and just I knew, by the colour of her apron, it was *her*.
> I walked in and told my sister.
> There was a nurse on the island — she's dead and gone now — I used to bring milk over to her. And I told her what I've seen.
> 'My God,' she says, 'she was only buried two days and I saw her coming over from the church and a candle in her hand. I've seen her twice.'

> One night I was up. Waiting for the cow to calve. And the cows we usually have, ye have to watch through.

And I took a walk away up to the statue [of the Virgin Mary in a grotto] up here, and I walked over to the head of the pier.

And I saw the image of a person coming over, very, very tall, and I recognised that person.

And in the English language I said 'Good night.' No reply. And I spoke in Irish. And I followed that person.

She was wearing a black coat and a black hat, and I *walked* hurriedly.

And, coming to a certain house in the town, I put my arms around her and my arms came back and I got terribly heated up.

So I walked up home, and I told my son that I wasn't keeping well and liked to go to bed, and that I'm not going to get up. I told my son, the cow she may not calve tonight, so *I* went to bed.

About eight o'clock the following April on a Sunday night, word came from the lighthouse that *this* [same] *lady* died in Scotland.

And that was true.

Now.

Another friend of mine, and nobody knows what happened to him, as he was lost for seven years.

And I was sleeping in my bedroom. And many's the time I used to look up the Bog Road seeing would I see anything. Or a face.

And on this particular night about half two, I saw this man coming out from his own garden, and he went up to his *own field*.

And, it was real quick, that I knew right away, that it was him.

He was wearing his suit, and a certain type of cap he had. And I turned to run from the bedroom, but there was not a soul to be seen.

Well, myself and a friend of mine was up at my grandfather's house years ago, 1940, in the month of February, or March.

And it was an old house, the timber was down but another portion of the house was standing substantial, we were chopping the timbers just for fire then.

And we could hear the footsteps of a person walking, up in this house. And we got heated up, and we didn't open the door.

The Dixon brothers of Tory told Seán Ó hEochaidh, when he was collecting folk tales on the island, of several things seen or experienced by the old people long ago. One was fairy boats, sometimes with a full crew, sailing on land; the other was 'air shots', stones that would come down out of the air and were supposed to have been shot from fairy guns. Pádraig Óg told me, 'As a young boy, the age of fourteen [1918], I saw the vision of a boat going over, coming from the west coast, it came direct from the pier. And I've been looking ever since for whatever it was.' I wish I had asked Pádraig more about it, but I did not know him well then and did not wish to interrupt again the flow of his stories. His description of the fairy shots was in much more detail.

When we were married, my wife and I used to take a walk over to the east end very often.

And this particular night she said that she would like to go down to the sea, as she came from a place in Belfast called Brougham. Close to the harbour. We were down there till one o'clock.

And a stone had been fired from the top of the hill, and *I* thought it was some person I knew that was doing it for devilment.

And some way and another while we were walking, on the *east* side of the harbour where the cliff was, about four or five stones came down.

I said, 'We'd better make for home.'

And we walked up, and when we were just at the very top, coming in to the main road, you would imagine that a *cave* fell, and it was a *bomb* or something had happened.

And we never we never said one word, and we didn't murmur either, until we come over to the village.

'Well,' I said, 'You'll never again go down there.' And I told her about the fairies.

One night, my wife and I took a walk. Nineteen forty two in the month of April, round by the lighthouse and down by the old Lloyd's station [at the west end].

And we stood there for a while talking.

And honest to God, you could hear the *echoes*. The echo of stones. Going like shots, around this house.

And we came around, and we made a very good search for fear some people would be throwing the stones, and no one to be seen.

So, we walked then direct back home.

* * *

There are several signs on Tory that are said to portend death: the sweet scent of perfume, the smell of tobacco, lights flickering in the gable ends of houses and the sound of crying. Pádraig's daughter, Eilish, told me that she was standing at the sink in her kitchen one morning when a strong scent of perfume wafted through the partly open window. A few days later, news came of her mother's death in Belfast. The smell of tobacco is considered a definite omen due, no doubt, to the traditional use of tobacco at a wake. Pádraig Óg remembers:

Now. My sister and I smelled wake, smell of tobacco, before this presently happened. And Annie said to me, 'We'll soon have a wake.'

And this is as true as God is in heaven, And we never thought more of anything.

And on this morning this great friend of mine was drowned on a boat coming from the mainland.

He was drunk and slipped over, and they made *every* effort to save him but all their efforts were in vain.

* * *

After distilling a successful batch of poteen, it was the custom to spill a few drops of it on the ground for the fairies. This was true also after taking a drink of the finished product or even after tasting 'legal' whiskey. If one did not, the angry fairies took revenge in a variety of crafty ways. The tale of the fisherman on Tory who did not throw out a drop is an old one and was told to me by both Jimmy Sarah Rodgers and Gráinne Bhrianaí Doohan. According to Gráinne, her father was in the boat when it happened:

> They were out in the country [mainland] with fish. And they were coming in and they had a bottle of whiskey, bought, with them. So everyone took a sip *out* of it. Till this old man who was at the steering. And they sent over the bottle to him to get a taste out of it.
> And the other man said to him, 'Throw out a drop to the fairies, now when we're halfway in.'
> 'Damn the drop,' says he; and the bottle fell out of his hand and smashed the whole lot. He didn't get nothing out of it. Well, that could happen, d'ye see.

When I first transcribed Pádraig's story of his misadventure in the graveyard on the night of the dance, I thought that the reason he became so terribly worried was that he had forgotten to give the fairies a taste of his whiskey. I realised, however, when I re-read it that he had indeed spilled the required drop, and came to the conclusion that his worry may have been the result of his dead mother's strong displeasure at his indulgence in drink at all.

> One night there's a dance in the school, not in the hall. That would be 1929.
> And, I got a bottle of whiskey. I was out to hide it and I went into the graveyard. And I hid the bottle there. The system [his parents] was very hard on you, they didn't want me taking anything to drink...
> And when I dressed myself at home I walked over, and I had a flash [light]. And I went *in* to the graveyard. And I got the bottle, a five-noggin bottle, and a glass.

And I had a corkscrew with me, a very nice corkscrew, and I unscrewed the cork on the tomb of a man called Seán Rodgers. In the graveyard. In this particular place.

And when I took the glass, the first glass I got there's an old saying that the poor usually want drink, and I turned around on that.

I *took* two glasses, right away in succession then, one after the other, and then I got another glass again and I put it on [drank it], that's *three* glasses.

I put the cork in the bottle, and just, I looked around, seeing my poor mother's grave.

And I said to myself, '*God* save us in this world sad and weary, when the day will come on me, when I'll be stretched the same way as my mother.'

And whatever really happened it came very, very quick that I got terribly *worried*. And I got afraid, and I left the bottle down, flung the bottle down and the glass, and the flash.

And if I *tumbled* once I tumbled about forty times as I went to the gate of the graveyard.

On my way coming — I had a new suit on — *oh,* I was knocked about, you know. I was knocked about.

And I met a certain man and I told him I have the flash, he went in and he *got my* flash. And the bottle, and the glass, and the corkscrew. And I came *back* home.

* * *

I was interested in the difference between keening and the kind of crying that was heard — as Pádraig Óg tells later — 'under the cart' or 'in the garden' or 'under the foot', the kind of crying that could move from one place to another. I asked Gráinne Bhrianaí Doohan about it, and if the crying was done by banshees. She avoided a direct answer. 'There was a wake on here, a young man died. And me and Mary Rodgers, Mary McClafferty now you call her, we were up at that wake. And about three o'clock that night we heard that crying. Out behind this house where the wake was. Just the tune, *lonely* tune, and it would make you cry.' I told her that Pádraig Óg spoke of hearing the crying often. 'That's right. Well, it was in that house. You can say that. The crying was in that house long, long ago, up in the old house where Paul is building the boat. We heard that when we were young. Aye. Pádraig Óg's mother died that time, so we thought it was her crying. Whether it was or not. Well, that's gone from here. You never hear that now on Tory.'

I was given a description of rather terrifying crying, however, that was heard not more than sixteen years ago. It was told to me by Patsy Dan's wife, Kathleen, a woman not easily upset. It was before they were married and Patsy, at that time, was taking the mail from the post office to the lighthouse. On a lovely moonlit night, he and Kathleen went to the lighthouse and, after delivering the letters, started to walk to Derek Hill's hut, on the cliffs of the north east, where they were supposed to meet two friends. As they walked towards the ruins of Lloyd's house, Kathleen 'got the shivers, I didn't want to go'. But they saw the light of a cigarette by the door of the hut and went on. Kathleen tells the story:

> So we went up anyway, when we looked, they weren't there at all, so we came round as far as the door. And we were just standing there about five minutes — here comes the dark. It was a *lovely* moonlit night, you could see everything very clear; and in five minutes it was all in darkness.
>
> And no way could you make your way down in that. Anyway, I said to Patsy, 'We'd better crawl.' We were afraid of our life we were going off the cliffs, the hut is so near the cliffs.
>
> So we went down on our knees and crawled. And we done that maybe for five minutes — *and here comes the crying*. Ohh, the wildest thing I ever heard. It was terrible. It seemed to come in from the sea; I thought so anyway.
>
> And the more they [the cliffs] were coming closer, it was coming nearer and nearer and nearer, like it was standing beside us. It was like something you would hear long ago at a funeral.

> And it was strange, when we came to the red railing [at the top of steep steps leading down to Greenport] it cleared again, there was moonlight. But the crying was with us all the time until we came down to the top of the lane and, when we came close to the houses, it start fading away… I got so cold, when I think of it I still get the shivers.

Pádraig Óg heard the crying frequently, and usually became 'heated up' — Patsy Dan told me that when one felt very warm, at times like these, it meant that the ghost or fairy was very close by.

> I quite remember one night, my sister and I were in our own home. And my wife was away at the time.
> And, whatever way it happened, my sister said something to me, [that] my mother or my aunts would give us a sign, a spiritual sign, that things would go right.
> And, just as we murmured *these words*,
> under the cart we had outside of our window, the *crying* started.
> And the crying went up to my garden and crossed over, and went to the door where my aunt used to live. And it was still going on there.
> And my father died that following June.

> One night, my father and I were sleeping in the same bed. It's true as the holy picture is there.
> And about two o'clock in the morning, the crying started, and crying and crying and crying.
> And the minute I opened my mouth, the crying stopped. And that was true, Dorothy, as true as my sister was buried at the week…
> Now. And they were crying 'Follow me. Pádraig, Pádraig.' That's the truth now. And the time my mother died I took it very, very, very hard.

> And I heard my father saying that he was one night in a certain place on the island.

And he said that he heard a crying. And the *crying* was under his foot.

And the following day an unexpected victim *died*. Suddenly.

Another thing I heard my father telling me, many's a time. Supposing some of the relatives would be stormbound on the mainland. And there was no possibility of them coming back to the island. Due to the storm. Northerly wind.

What they would generally do, they would put three drops of water into their mouths, and they would take a bag, a sack, like, and they would open the bag. And they would face the bag to the lee side so that the wind would blow in their favour the following day.

They would go to the cliff and pray hard, that the wind would go to the south, so that the boat will come.

And that had been done many's a time. And that was genuine. That was true. Certainly, Dorothy.

* * *

When Alfred McFarland visited Paddy Heggarty, 'the resident Sovereign', on Tory in 1849, he spoke of Heggarty's sister, 'the Princess Nelly, a dark-eyed and merry lass of some fifteen years or more', but made no mention of the king's wife. The 'king' indeed had a wife, although perhaps at that time she had gone to live on the mainland, or may even have died. According to Hugh Curran of Gortahork, 'Local lore says she was a Magheraroarty woman, six feet tall, which helps to explain the story of their wedding day. They were married in Gortahork and, afterwards, raced the incoming tide across the strand on their way to Magheraroarty. However, at a river channel, the approaching tide left the passage too deep for His Majesty. So the bride placed him — him being so small — in her apron and ferried him over.' They had two small daughters, one of them, Máire Phaidí (Máire Bheag, as Pádraig called her), lived in Magheraroarty. Hugh Curran remembered her as being so small that she could not look over the counter of the shop, but she was 'finely boned and perfectly formed'. The other daughter, 'a midget as well', ran a speakeasy in Bristol, Pennsylvania. One afternoon, as I sat across from Pádraig Óg beside the fire, I asked him if he would tell me something about Paddy Heggarty; it seemed an eminently appropriate subject.

> Well, Paddy Heggarty, he was a schoolteacher here, and himself and the priest had a fall[ing] out. They fell out over some *matter*.
> And Paddy Heggarty was living, as far as I know, was out in the east end. He was married.
> Now. Paddy Heggarty made up his mind, on account of this complication between himself and the priest, and the confusion — he didn't approve of the attitude the priest had adopted.
> And he left Tory Island. And he went down to Co Antrim, down to Ballycastle and in to Rathlin Island.
> And he commenced to teach there on Rathlin Island, and he was a Catholic when he was here and he converted into the Protestant religion down in Rathlin Island, Co Antrim.
> And he died, *as* a Protestant, on Rathlin Island.
> And that's all I can say about him.
> Strange to say, I met his daughter, Máire Bheag, as small as about three or four feet in height.
> And many's the shilling I used to give her out.
> She was born in a place called The Lane, out in Magheraroarty, out here in Donegal, out here. And she died out at Magheraroarty.
> Now. Ever since Paddy died, they had no recognised king of the island. The only person then that they were recognising was Séamus Ward of Tory Island.
> He was what you would call, officially, locally appointed, but just they give him the distinction, like, that he would be a king.
> And Séamus Ward then left Tory Island, the first champion step-dancer in all Ireland, in his day, and a Gaelic League organiser for years and years. And a powerful strong man.

And the island did miss him greatly

But in any case, when *he* left Tory Island then, people came to me and they said 'Well let's put Pádraig Óg,' and they gave me the distinction that they would have me as the king of the island.

Which has no remuneration attached, only just the name and the fame. Just as I was writing for them. And I did oblige them.

And I quite remember, in the month of August, 1914, Roger Casement came to the island with a crowd from Dublin.

Now. Ward's have the licence for, oh, twenty years.

But due to the fact, that fishing trawlers from Fleetwood and Grimsby used to come in here to the harbour and come in to the island,

the *community* didn't approve of the latitude they were adopting in certain personal matters

which I'm not going to divulge.

The priest then came to Jimmy [Ward], and he says that he wants that licence to be dropped. So, he gave up the licence. Got rid of it. And there was no more whiskey to be sold on the premises of Ward.

Well, Niall Ward, that's Séamus Ward's father, I suppose he would be recognised as the King of Tory.

Because they had a lovely estate there. You wouldn't get the like of it in all Ireland.

Had a lovely residential place for visitors, the same as a hotel.

And he had a lovely *field*. And, if you went up to the cliff and looked down, when Ward's premises were in full *bloom* you would be full of admiration.

You wouldn't get the like of it in many parts of Ireland and that's the God's honest truth.

That all stopped, Ward's shop closed down then; not for *many*, many years did sister Ellie Ward get the shop going, she kept the shop going, oh, twenty-five years after that. It was closed then and more or less part of it is demolished now. It was a great pity.

* * *

Pádraig had a little more schooling than most of the islanders of his day. As far as I know, he did not have to leave the Tory national school to work on the land and so, as a promising scholar, was able to remain in class until the age limit of fourteen. He spent a brief period, after this, at a national school on the mainland and then did a home study course with Hughes Academy, a college in Derry. The following year he became registrar of births, deaths and marriages on Tory. Pádraig may have been a promising scholar but this did not prevent him from skipping school, whenever possible, like the other boys.

> I went to school when I was four years. In 1908.
>
> Now, when I went to school, I hated school. And so did my brother Bernard that died out in America.
>
> We used to hide up the cliffs, and we'd be watching the scholars when they would be coming out in the school year, and join their company. In order to avoid trouble.
>
> I used to be hiding, but all the teachers here used to give me lessons, home lessons at night. And, well, I don't know, I was *gifted*.
>
> I had great intelligence and I was very dapper — in the education *sphere*, like — and the teachers said that if my parents could afford to send me to college for a while,
>
> that I would be a *genius*.
>
> But circumstances did not permit. Because times were very hard on Tory Island as regards the livelihood. Out fishing ten miles from the island in open, frail boats; fishing cod and ling.

The cat, lying under a settee nearby, had been coughing. Now it began to cough in a distressing way. 'There's something the matter with its throat,' said Pádraig. 'It's been doing this for a while. It's sick.' Getting to his feet, he gave the cat a gentle nudge with his cane and shooed it towards the door. 'Come, Puss, Puss, Puss, Puss, Pussy, Pussy,' he encouraged, until it had disappeared over the threshold. When he came back into the room, the thread of the conversation had been broken. I left the subject of schooling and asked him what the houses on Tory were like when he was young.

> They were *all* thatched, except the room in my grandfather's house. It was slate. And to say the truth about them, they were far healthier than the slated house. That's the truth now.
> I certainly admit, on my own conscience,
> that the people went before me.
> They probably did penance in this world,
> *in* comparison
> *with,*
> the improvements of Tory at the present time.
> But Tory Island improved, so much economically now, that we don't realise that we are living on Tory at *all*. It got so modern in every way.
> The people at that time, on Tory Island, and on Inishtrahull, and on many parts of the *mainland too*, they had only from the hand to the mouth. There was no money, the way it is now. Listen here.
> Tory and the islands now, they are gold mines in comparison with the young days. I know it myself. And I am very, very proud, and very glad, how well that things are with the present time, on this island.
> And there is one thing I have to say.
> Prominent people came to this island, very distinguished people. My friend de Valera, and Lord Leitrim and the whole outfit came. I quite remember that myself.
> I quite remember the Earl of Leitrim coming here... Oh, I quite remember that myself. He came here, a nice person.
> And de Valera, and President Childers, he was here, but not officially.

* * *

Pádraig had described the difficult life the fishermen had and I asked him one afternoon about the old currachs, the kind that were made by stretching hide over a frame of basket work. I remembered that Dónal Doohan had sung a song for me, 'An Bhó Chrúbach' ('The cow with turned-in horns'); it is well-known on Tory as the 'Ballad of Éamon Ó Dubhagáin's Cow' and was written by Jimmy Duggan's grandfather in the days when this type of currach was in use. The song tells of Éamonn Ó Dubhagáin who went out to a fair in Falcarragh and bought a cow from a man from Ranafarste, in the Rosses. He took the cow into Tory, but it was not long before the cow died. He kept the hide and made a currach in which he went fishing in Camusmore. But one night a gale came up, the currach was torn from its mooring and was carried away by the winds. 'Was it funny,' Dónal asked me, 'when they got the currach in the *same place* what the cow came from? The place they call Ranafarst.' Pádraig Óg said:

> Well, them old currachs, you know, they had no keels; they used to go with a *paddle* instead of the oars. So they invented this new type, four oars; that's the latest type of currach that has been made on Tory. The old ones, they wouldn't go to the mainland.
>
> But there was *one* man named Denis Diver, he went *over,* and he landed in Dunfanaghy [more than ten miles] with his currach in the morning and he came back the same evening again with the currach. That would be Jimmy Diver's great-grandfather. I heard that. Oh, that was true.

* * *

If there was, as Pádraig Óg once referred to it as, a 'recognised' cursing stone now hidden somewhere on the western end of the island, there is a very visible wishing stone at the east end. It stands on a ledge that juts out several feet from the cliff, just far enough to make it difficult to throw a small stone onto it and have it stay there. It is triangular in shape, about two or three feet wide at its top and narrowing to a base that is, as Dan Rodgers says, 'just the size of my fist'. It would take someone with a strong stomach, and a strong faith, to stand on it. Alfred McFarland wrote, 'As the common rumour goes, if one but walk round it three times, he has only to express the desire of his heart, no matter what, and it will be accomplished.' Whether one stands or walks on the wishing stone, however, I am in total agreement with the opinion of McFarland's companion on the Tory trip, 'that... it might be seen by anyone who had half an eye, that nothing except a goat could make the circuit in safety — and he would be a goat that tried it.' The sea lies very far below. Pádraig Óg told me about it.

> Now.
> I stood on the wishing stone five times myself. *I stood up on the wishing stone.*
> But the way you had to make the wish is that you'll get three stones.
> And prior to making your wish, you stand on the earth on the cliff. And you throw on the stones like that. If the three stones remain on the rock, you'll get your wish, and if one falls, you will not get it. That's the truth now.
> And now listen to me.
> The first day I was a fisherman — I used to fish long ago, that's before I start using the pen — I came around. And, from the sea, I looked up where the wishing stone was.
> And to tell you the truth, my heart went like that. I was just thinking what would be the consequence. The stone, the way it is, would frighten you and this stone, according to the old tradition, this stone will never go,
> unless some human person goes with it.
> That has been said a hundred years ago. Not a hundred, but *hundreds*. That's an old saying on the rock.
> And I got my wish on the wishing stone three times. And five times, *five* times I stood on the rock.
> When my father and mother heard, my father and mother nearly killed me here. They got a sea-rod to beat me, to warn me.

I used to climb the cliffs very often in my young days. But they wouldn't let me over to the east end for a long, long, long time.

That's the truth now.

* * *

Now.

My mother went to America at the age of sixteen. And she was only out in America two years, when a letter came to her, that her only brother died with the measles. And her sister Bridget.

Both were buried the same day on this island.

And my mother then came back, d'ye know, and she remained here for a year, and she went back then to America. And spent three or four years there. She was a priest's maid.

She came back here and she met my father and they got married and settled down here.

My mother was a great cook. One of the *best* in Ireland, that's the truth I'm going to say. And she won first prize, as a girl, for the beauty of her hands, that's the truth.

Well, my father was a very prudent man. He had a little education. He wasn't what you call professed or anything like that. He was never in college. Much better.

But he had great brains and he could visualise the aspect of things ahead,

which I didn't.

Now. My father was a carpenter. And he worked hard in his day, both on sea and land. If I would [have] take[n] his advice in my day — I didn't, but there's no use talking.

And he used to build houses on the east end for the Congested Districts Board, or the Land Commission. And he built *this* house at his own expense.

And long ago, when there was no parochial house on Tory Island, all the priests that ever came, they roomed, here.

Oh, there were very few houses on Tory Island that were able to accommodate people *then*.

But now they have *hotels*. That's the truth.

You get fed up listening to them, what they're talking about now. That's the truth. But in the olden days, they weren't able to do it.

And I was very, very proud of my father. He used to build boats. And my grandfather was a carpenter too. He fished and he would have to put out sea-rods, putting out the seaweed, making kelp, so as to be able to maintain himself and his wife.

And it was my grandfather that made a song, in Irish: Níl Sé 'na Lá' they call it in Irish.

'It's not the morning' — Níl Sé 'na Lá'.

The following, in Pádraig Óg Rodgers' handwriting, is the ballad written by his grandfather on Tory Island. It was translated for me by Maureen Rodgers of Tory, in September, 1986.

It's not Morning

Chorus:
It's not morning, it's not, my love,
It's not morning,
And it won't be for a while,
The moonlight is still high in the sky

I went into a house last night,
And I asked the barmaid for a whiskey,
She said to me, 'You'll not get one drop.
Get out on the road and go home.'

Chorus

I put my hand in my pocket,
And I asked her for the change of a sovereign.
She said to me, 'Give me your order,
And keep drinking here till morning.'

Chorus

> *Oh, man of the house arise,*
> *Put on your trousers and your hat,*
> *And play your music for this honest man,*
> *Who will be drinking here till morning.*
>
> Chorus

* * *

I took my tape recorder to Pádraig's house several times in the following years, and asked many questions. One of them, of course, was about St Colmcille and why and how he had come to Tory. Dónal Doohan said that the saint 'come out in a currach one day'; William Rodgers spoke only of some of his prophecies; Dan Rodgers told me, 'When Colmcille landed on the Muckish [a mountain lying some miles inland from Falcarragh], he fired his stick to Tory.' Pádraig's version was that Colmcille 'flung his crutch' from Horn Head. He continued with the usual account of the saint's coming to the island, 'at that time *packed* with evil spirits'; of his 'putting up a monastery in order to form a certain doctrine to teach the true faith to the people'; of the holy clay and the Duggans, and of the cursing stone.

> Now. When St Colmcille came to Tory, he blessed Tory, he blessed Tory. And he banished the druids. Put them over the cliffs.
>
> According to the old tradition — I don't know whether it's legitimate or not — but from what I heard from the elderly people, St Colmcille called it Oileán Cholmcille, 'St Colmcille's Island'.
>
> And we still maintain that word yet.
>
> No matter in all my travels, in the many parts of Ireland I went to, when I was asked where did I come from, I said Oileán Cholmcille, 'St Colmcille's Island'.
>
> That's from the old people; the old people used to tell me that. And that was true. ■

Gráinne Bhrianaí Doohan
(b. 1916)

It was Mary McClafferty who suggested that I talk to Gráinne Bhrianaí Doohan. When I first began recording she was spending a certain amount of time on the mainland and I did not know her very well. Patsy Dan introduced us on one of her visits home to Tory, and I remembered her as a friendly person, standing with the aid of a walker at the door of her house, facing the bay. Soon afterwards she had a successful operation on her arthritic hip and she and her husband Patrick were able to stay for longer periods on the island. When Mary said that I should go to see her, I felt a little embarrassed at the thought of walking into an unfamiliar house with a tape recorder. But I did go to see Gráinne — without a tape recorder the first time — and realised at once that my worry about imposing on her was unfounded. Gráinne, the mother of six — five boys and 'wee Gráinne' who died at the age of two — has an easy smile, twinkling eyes and a lilting voice. She welcomed me into the house and we took our seats on either side of the fire. My chair faced the window with a view that became very familiar during my ensuing visits. From it I could see the soft brown of the pier; the surrounding bay; the comings and goings of the Tory half-deckers; and further glimpses of some of the whitewashed houses of East Town — a lovely view, especially on a clear afternoon when the sun made silver ripples on the bright blue water.

I asked Gráinne if she would be willing to tell me a bit about her life. Perhaps, I suggested, she could begin with some of the stories she heard from her mother. She seemed pleased. 'There's one,' she said, 'that I won a prize for in a story-telling contest in the country, but I told it in Irish. It won't be as good in English.

Would you like to hear it?' 'I would indeed,' I replied, regretting immediately that, out of what then seemed a misguided sense of politeness I had not brought the recorder with me. This had happened to me before, and sometimes the stories, when repeated for the tape recorder, did not have quite the same spontaneity. When I returned the next day, however, Gráinne's story had lost none of its charm. She told an old-fashioned fairy-tale about a king and his queen, who had been banished unjustly due to the schemes of a jealous sister-in-law, and of their own two children, reared by an old fisherman and his wife, unaware of their royal heritage. It all ended with everyone living happily every after, the villain having been thrown into a barrel of boiling tar as a just reward for her wickedness. Gráinne told me that this tale and many more that had been found by her uncle among books salvaged from boats wrecked along the Tory coast. During my visits, I was treated to several other equally delightful stories.

However, as my yearly trips to Tory continued, I became interested in the remedies and cures that were used in the days when there was no nurse on the island and a doctor was hard to come by. I asked about old potions, poultices and embrocations, and was told about a variety of plants, gathered in the fields, that were effective both internally and externally. No one knew their names expect for the common nettle which, when boiled and made into a most unsavoury soup, caused the measle rash to 'come out'. Jimmy Duggan, from East Town, described his father's method of getting rid of 'dust or rust' in the eye: Take a clean white plate and put it on a chair or table. Wash your mouth out well with water. Then take a fresh sip of water and holding it in your mouth, say a certain long prayer. When the prayer is finished, spit the water out onto the plate. The dust, or rust will appear on the plate and the irritation will leave your eye. Kathleen Rodgers, while rubbing brandy gently, and successfully, on her colicky baby's stomach, told me the way to get rid of general aches and pains, bad eyes or dangerous warts. One must get up between twelve and two in the morning, she said, and go the baptismal font near the tower; there is always water in the font and some of this should be applied to the affected spot.

Unfortunately, the cure won't work if anybody is met along the way. Warts, either dangerous or benign, seemed to be a frequent affliction. A piece of meat or white bacon, left under a rock, was usually effective; as the meat rotted, the warts disappeared. One of the most popular cures was accomplished by the transference of one's own warts to someone else. This was done by making up a small enticing parcel. Its contents varied from bits of broken matches, equalling the number of warts, to the 'nicest white threepenny piece with a picture of a rabbit on it right enough, long ears and all', found by Peggy Rodgers. These packets were left by the roadside to be picked up by the curious, and naïve, traveller. The warts accompanied the packet.

Gráinne contributed much to my knowledge of old Tory remedies, and her mother, I learned quickly, had her own particular way of curing various ailments. Warts were no exception.

> She used corn. There's wee nuts on corn, up to six or seven on each. My mother used to cut them with a scissors and rub them around the wart. Three days. And then put them under a stone.
>
> She would say as long as they were rotting, the warts would be going away from your hand. Other people used to put them in a small bag and fire them out on the road so that somebody would catch them. But my mother never did that.

There was no need for Gráinnes's mother to walk, in the early hours of the morning, to the baptismal font for water to apply to sore eyes. She kept the first-laid egg of the pullet, which was recognisable by the 'wee taste of blood on it' and she would make the sign of the cross three times on each eye, for three days. 'She would keep the egg,' said Gráinne, 'till the whole family done with it, and never we got a stye on the eye.'

> And wait till I tell you now.
> My mother used to have a cure, for old people that would be complaining.

This is the way I know it — my mother's sister and a friend of hers were over in our house one winter's night. And this woman was complaining of her heart.

And my mother said to her, 'Well,' she said, 'I'll make you this cure for it. *If* you decide to do it.'

'Oh, yes,' says she.

'Well,' said my mother, 'go down on your knees there now,' says she.

And she went into the room and she got a bit — about eighteen inches long — of brown flannel. And she cut *three* woollen, white threads, and she spread them on it, and she folded it up tight. And she put it in beside the woman's heart. And my mother started praying.

And she took it out then and she put it around three times under her arms, and three times around her head. And she put it back again.

So she started saying a few more prayers, and then she took it out. And she put it on the table and spread it out. And one of the cords was short.

And my mother said, 'You're not *so* bad *with it*, but a little.'

And she folded it back again and she put it back in. And she said, 'You have to go out to the back of the house with me now. And lie down on the green grass.'

And my mother put a wee stone at her feet and a wee stone at her head.

And she got a spade, and she dug up a wee piece of the green stuff, of the sod and she told her to put her breath down there three times.

So she did that. And she got better.

[Gráinne warmed to the subject.]

And the shingles, now. Well

Out in Ballina it was Madge Rodgers that had the shingles. And Peggy [Madge's daughter-in-law] met a woman up at the bingo [hall] and she was telling her about the old woman was sick.

She says, 'Maybe it's the shingles she has?'

'Well,' Peggy said, 'how is that?'

She says, 'Your body will be covered with wee red spots *all* around you.'

'Well, that's the same way she is,' says Peggy.

'I have the cure,' she says.

'Well by God, you're the one I want,' says Peggy.

'Well, tomorrow morning,' she says, 'I'll be there.'

So she came with a rooster. And she took the scissors and took one of the things off the head of the rooster. And took the blood out of it and she put the blood *all around* her, where she had the wee red spots.

And the next morning she came again and done the same thing — for three days. And she got better.

Usually, while applying a remedy, a prayer or two was said, a Hail Mary or an Our Father. I asked if a prayer was used with the remedy of the rooster's blood. 'Oh, there's no prayers for that,' Gráinne said firmly. 'And there's another cure [without prayer] was here. You had to get up at six o'clock in the morning and go to this man on the east end. And he had a sixpence with a hole in it, and put it on where you had the sore part. Three mornings, too.'

My father, for the whooping cough, used to bring in an' old donkey. There weren't many donkeys on this island at that time, but my father's uncle had one.

So he caught it one day — we had the whooping cough — and my mother was standing on this side and my father on the other, and my mother would put the baby around under.

Three times, under the donkey.

My father would catch it this side and she would catch it that side.

And she would give a bit of bread to the donkey. And the crumbs that would fall out of the donkey's mouth, she would catch it and put it into the baby's mouth.

There was another cure here, if you broke your *arm*, anybody broke his arm, there was a man here [that] when he was born his mother gave him a bone, put a bone in his hand.

And he would have that cure.

Jimmy Diver there, he used to. He died long ago.

And another woman over in the east end, Kate Meenan, she had it. If you give a baby a bone in his hand, they would always have the cure then.

And a boy that would be born with his legs coming first [breech birth], you know. Babies born like that can cure a back. Just three steps on the top of the back. Three times, three days. Everything was three days.

There was no prayer for that; just the name of the Father, the Son, and the Holy Ghost.

If you take a pain in here, between the two bones here — *cliath mhochán* [the two edges of the rib cage], we call it, an Irish name, d'ye see — my mother used to get a glass. And a penny and a bit of a candle stuck in the penny, and put the glass on top of it.

And if you *had* that pain, it would swell up into the glass. And the glass would stick to you. And you have to keep it there for about five or six minutes. It takes the pain away.

You had to do it three mornings. I did it myself, the time I had a pain here. I did it myself in my bed. Aye, that's right.

And the sore mouth, sore tongue.

Someone would be born that never saw his father. Born after his father died. He would breathe into your mouth three mornings. And it would go away.

Well, I got that done myself.

* * *

In the well-known fairy stories on Tory — found, as well, in many parts of Donegal — the theme remains the same although the location and some of the events leading to the particular experience may differ. Gráinne told me her version of a popular Tory fairy-tale as she heard it from her uncle.

> Well, the tobacco was very scarce on this island at that time. And they used to go out on the back of the island to get tobacco from big ships.
>
> So this man got a *tin* of tobacco. And everybody was asking for it, so he hid it. He went over and hid it in a hole over at the cliffs.
>
> And when everybody was going to bed, this night, he thought he would want some of it. He went in the dark for fear anybody would see him.
>
> And he went where the tobacco was and he got the tobacco. And after hiding the rest of it again, and taking with him some of it, when he was getting up he saw this light.
>
> He didn't know what kind of light it was, so when he's coming near it, it was a house.
>
> He said to himself, 'I wonder under God whose is that house.' So, he went over to the door and he heard the terrible [wonderful] music going. Dancing and singing.
>
> He opened the door slowly. The house was full. He sat down inside the door and there was a red-haired woman there. And she said to the fellow, 'If they offer you anything, don't take it. If they offer you a drink, don't take it.'
>
> And he looked up at her and she was watching him. She said, 'If you do, you'll be here the rest of your life.'
>
> So he got afraid then. And there was an old man sitting in the corner with a pipe in his mouth, and the fellow said he had a white beard down to here.
>
> He got afraid then and walked out. And when he went outside there was no house at all.
>
> And my uncle told me there was here a man had a fiddle and he used to be playing every evening with it. But he died, and left the fiddle in the house after he died.

> And every evening at seven o'clock, the fiddle used to play a tune.
> And many's a time my uncle told me he was listening to it. When they were wee.

Some fairies may appear as people, others in the form of animals such as rabbits and black cats. Still others wish to remain invisible, such as the *slua sí*, the fairy host, who pass overhead like a whirlwind; like the fairies who were hammering nails into a coffin for Dónal Doohan's grandmother the day before she died; or like those who fire air-shots, with stones, from fairy guns. According to Gráinne the air-shots are a sign of death and she and her mother heard them the time her mother's cousin died in Derry.

> We were sitting at the fire. We had a pot of poundings [mashed potatoes] on the fire, that time. And this handful of gravel was thrown, as if it would be thrown down from top of the house. Down on the door.
> And my mother got up and there was nothing there. And we were just sitting down when that happened again. Twice.
> My mother said, 'I'm going to hear bad news. That's the sign,' she said, 'of bad news.' It was true.

> And wait till I tell you this one.
> I was sitting in this house — before my uncle died, that's forty years he's buried now. My brother, Patrick, wasn't married at all. He was going to the east end, he was meeting Mary Doherty at the time.
> And me and Willy — the one that's out in the country — was sitting there and he said to me, 'Look at the time it is, and Patrick didn't come *yet*.'
> Says I, 'It's after twelve o'clock. He's not afraid,' says I, 'that the wee man that's over at the torpedo will come on him.' They used to say there was a *fairy* there.
> So, Willy went home and I was sitting there and here comes Patrick. And I said to him, 'Aren't you out late,

coming on to one o'clock and you over so late on the east.'

'Ah,' he said, that's *damn* nonsense you're talking about.'

As he said the word ['damn'], here comes this, like a 'glassoon' — ye know things for making the wind — *vroo*, down the chimney. It came down the chimney. And all the soot. And it fired me over from the stool.

And this big black lump, came and went over here and down in the corner.

My brother ran like anything out the door. And *I* ran. I didn't put off the light itself. I was that much afraid.

And I told the priest about it. Fr Duggan, you call him, he's dead long ago. And I said to him I was very shocked about it. And what it was.

'Well,' he said to me, 'that was the fairy was passing at the time you were talking about it,' he said.

'Maybe,' he said, 'you shouldn't be talking about evil spirits at that hour of the night,' he said. 'You should be in your bed.'

Sir William Wilde wrote that the flight of the fairy host, passing unseen overhead, occurs whenever the host 'venture abroad or suddenly change their residence in the open day...' And he was told also by many people that they had 'heard and *felt* the fairies pass them with a sound like that of a swarm of bees, or a flock of sparrows on the wing'.

The *slua sí* on Tory flew in a whirlwind of music, laughter and gibberish. Jimmy Rodgers Sarah told me that, years ago, when the islanders were gathering sea-wrack on the shore in the evening, they would leave their work as soon as they heard the sound of the fairy gibberish approaching from the sea. Gráinne herself had never heard the *slua sí*, but her aunt had.

Aye. My auntie heard the *slua sí*. A *whole lot*, of gibberish. Talking and talking but you wouldn't understand a word they were saying.

There was a mission here on Tory, long, long ago,

when she was only thirteen. And she stayed in with the
baby. Everybody was over at the chapel at Devotions,
when she heard this music and singing coming.

She come out here, and it passed down over there,
down by the pier, down the shore. The singing and the
music. Up as far as the chapel it went. And she heard
them talking but she didn't see nobody,
she didn't see nobody.

She was *enjoying* the music. She had no sense. But she
was afraid too, for she went up next door to the old
woman that was in the house, and told her.

But they won't go near you anyway. They won't touch
you.

Five or six years ago, Gráinne's son heard laughing and
talking outside the kitchen window while he and a friend were
making poteen. He went out and looked everywhere but there
was no one to be seen. Yet as soon as he went back to the still the
noise began again. 'Well, it may not be the same,' said Gráinne,
'but they were talking and laughing *in beside* the window. And
you couldn't understand *one word* they were saying. So the boys
just catch the whole thing and fire the whole lot out, down the
shore. From that day to this day they never made poteen. That
finished them off.'

One afternoon, several days after my first visit to Gráinne, I
went again to her house, tape recorder in hand. The weather was
showery, the sea grey, the fire in the kitchen welcome indeed. It
seemed a good atmosphere for more stories of strange
happenings, and Gráinne's supply of them seemed limitless. Just
before we settled down to taping, Gráinne's son came in with his
two-month-old daughter, another 'wee Gráinne', and put her, in
her little carrying chair, on the floor between us. All during our
story-telling she lay there happily watching the fire, listening to
her granny's voice and occasionally making small *coo*ing sounds,
which added greatly to the charm of the finished tape.

A few days before Anton Duggan, that's my cousin,
got drowned, he was on his way from Downings in the
boat.

And in the middle of the ocean here comes this lovely *green leaf*. And it lay down beside him on the boat. A leaf from a tree. Out in the middle of the sea.

And he said to himself, 'That's the funniest thing I ever *saw*.'

He got up and tried to *catch* the leaf but when he catch the leaf there was no leaf there.

A week afterwards he was drowned.

He was telling that here to me. And little I thought he had only one week to live. A week, *just one week*, he was drowned.

But it was a funny kind of sign, wasn't it? A green leaf?

No tree out in the middle of the sea. That leaf came down from the sky and lay on the boat. But when he *catched* it there was no leaf. He was telling that to me. It's funny.

My mother's brother was drowned, when my sister was only a baby. And she was living up there at Lloyd's house, d'ye know, that house up at the lighthouse?

And my uncle used to be over there every night with her. So this night he didn't come.

And my father was down at the village. So she was sitting in at the fire and she was rocking my sister to sleep.

And she had a line of clothes up, hanging in the kitchen. And this sheet came down as somebody would *pull* it. And threw it over her head.

So she was wondering what happened. She got up and folded the sheet. And she went outside. And she saw this man coming.

And she said to him, 'Aren't you late tonight? What kept you?'

Nobody answered her. So she came in and she left the door open. And he came as far as the door, and she could hear his steps, *at* the door. But she went out and there was nobody there.

She said to herself, 'Where did he go?'

She went out and she came round that house. And she didn't see nobody. She came in back again. And she was all upset then. And she was waiting on my father to come.

She heard then, this whispering coming. She went out and it was my father. And his sister was up with him. My mother was wondering why he had his sister *up* with him, that time of night. And she said, 'What kept you?'

'Oh,' he said, 'your brother was fishing,' he said, 'and he hurt his leg, so I was over.'

At that time her brother was drowned. But she didn't know. He was drowned the time the sheet came down.

And she went to bed that night. Early that morning my father got up, and he said to my mother, 'You'd better get ready and go to see your brother.' He was afraid to tell her that he was drowned.

She got ready, and she came down as far as my granny down here. And my granny told her. She said, 'Your brother got drowned.' My mother collapsed.

And he was drowned five nights.

The *last* day of January they were saying Devotions in the house for the body to come ashore. And it was on Brigid's night, the *first* day of February, that his body was recovered.

And they had a wee boy that his mother died, my mother's sister, and she left the baby behind her as well.

And the wee boy was only eight years at that time. He was out, and he come in and he said to my mother, he said, 'There's a woman out at the window with a white gown. And a white shawl.'

My mother went out. My mother couldn't see it.

'*There* she is,' says he, 'she's around the corner.' And my mother went around. My mother didn't see nothing. But they were saying 'twas St Brigid.

And the next morning the body was washed ashore.

'I was asking you the other day,' I said, 'about the lights that were seen in the gables of the Diver house in the east, before

Wully Diver died. Does everyone on Tory see lights, and is it really a sign of death?'

> Well, some of them do, others don't. Oh, I saw it a few times.
> My wee girl was sick here. Wee Gráinne that died.
> And I went up to the lighthouse for a jar of oil, because oil was scarce at the time of the war. And Peggy Val with me — a wee girl — and coming over the road there I saw a light on the side of the road.
> I said to Peggy, 'Can you see that light?'
> 'Yes,' says she.
> Says I, 'That's funny, they say that's a death, when you see a light.' And I said to Peggy, 'The wee girl's going to die.'
> 'Ah,' she said, 'maybe that's nonsense.'
> But, when I came home, the wee girl only lasted two days. That was true.
>
> Well, the light is like that. You'll get the sign of the light. I got it on my auntie, too. Like a flash lamp flashing on the wall. She died the same night at two o'clock.
> I was talking to her and the light was up above her head on the wall. Oh, I saw it a few times. I saw it when my mother died as well.
> And another thing. The dead-watch! Did ye ever hear about that? The dead-watch. Going like a clock in the wall but you won't see it.
> Aye, it's the sign of death too. It's a terrible sign of death.
> Well, out in Inishbofin — wait till I tell you this now — out in Inishbofin out here, there's a house there and the death-clock is going there all the time. It's going there for a century, the death-clock.
> The people went to live in Glasgow for a while, and the clock went with them.

It was going in the cupboard over in Glasgow. And they came back again and *it* come back again.

And I heard it here. Oh, I did. I heard that when my granny died. It wakened me out of my sleep. In my bedroom, over at home that time.

I wakened my sister and I said to her, 'Did you hear that?'

Here the clock was *going*. And we had no clock, only the one was down in the kitchen.

And about three o'clock, there come a knock to the window. And it was my auntie. She said to my father, 'Are ye up? Barney, are ye up?'

'No.'

She said, 'My mother's after dying.' That was my granny. She died in 1934. It's a way back.

Speaking of death, I thought of wakes and funerals. 'Did women cry at the wake as well as at the graveyard?' I asked.

O, they cried their fill.

After the body will be fixed and dressed and back in the bed, they would cry then. They would cry their fill. And when it was buried, they would cry on top of the grave. They used to cry out loud, long ago, on Tory.

My mother was a terrible cryer. Anybody could sing, could cry lovely. Lovely singing, *lovely* crying. It sounded like — *talking* with the person that's dead. What had happened when they were together and things like that.

It's from the heart. It's kind of lonely. Crying a person that's dead is very lonely crying.

It's really kind of singing, you know, up and down. 'Ohhhh, my heart,' that was the way they start. 'I'll never see you again. Many's a day you came to visit me...' You know, that kind of way.

I can still hear my mother crying, 'I'll never see you again coming up the road. I'll never see you again going out in a boat. I'll never see you again going over to

Mass.' *All* them things. 'We'll never sit and chat again.' Make everybody cry. You wouldn't like to hear it.

But everybody was crying in the graveyard that time. Many's the crying was over in that old graveyard there.

When I was a wee girl, we used to be sitting over there listening to them cry. And we used to be practising from the old people how to cry. [Gráinne laughed.]

That time. When we were wee girls.

My father was going up to Greenport one morning. He was working up where Derek Hill's hut is now. And when he was passing Greenport, the rooster started crowing.

He stood listening to it, and it made *six* of them crows.

He said to himself, 'That's funny, there's no roosters up here.'

So he went up anyway.

The next morning there was a ship wrecked over on the east end, full of flour and things. The *Wheatplain*. We said it was a *caoi* [opportune] day. We said that in Irish, *caoi*, I can't put English on it.

God sent good things to the island. It was a good time.

* * *

Well, I'll tell you a story now about *myself*.

When I was about six years old, or seven, I was watching the baby for my mother, she went over shopping.

She said to me '*Don't you move out of the house* now till I come back. And watch the baby and the fire.'

So I went up on the table and I sat looking out of the window. And when I was looking here comes this kind of doll. And stood in front of me. With a red cloak and all design in silver.

I said to myself, 'Isn't that lovely.' And you could see

its feet, I could see its two wee feet, in under the cloak. And I could see its hands raising under it.

I said to myself, 'What under God is it anyway? And I wonder will it come over near the window.'

And *I* sat watching it till the baby started crying. And I went to make him shut up right away. When I went up again on the table, it was gone. And I told my mother and my mother wouldn't believe me at all. Till I went down to Derry to work. I was eighteen years old.

And I was passing the window. I said to my mother, '*That's* what I saw now when I was a little girl. There, it's in there.' The Child of Prague.

And I was *praying all the time* to get one of them. And one night there was a bazaar over in the schoolhouse here.

I *won* the Child of Prague. And I still have it.

Gráinne got up from her chair and went into the next room. When she returned she brought with her the small, painted ceramic statue of the Child of Prague to show me. The Child wore a crown and from under his long, red cloak, his little feet peeped out; his hand was raised.

The afternoon had not yet slipped away. The baby, in her carrying chair by the hearth, was happy. It seemed there was time enough. 'That was a lovely story,' I said. 'Perhaps you could tell me just one more, "one more and no more" as I used to say to my father when I was little and eating strawberries in the garden.' Gráinne laughed. 'What about the fairy that's supposed to be seen always at Portadoon?' I suggested.

Sir William Wilde wrote in 1852, 'The general belief... is that the "good people", or the "wee folk", as they are termed in Ulster, are *fallen angels* (the idea of their being fallen angels came in with Christianity) and that their present habitations in the air, in the water, or dry land, or under ground, were determined by the position which they took up when first cast from heaven's battlement.'

Aye. There was a man there, my uncle saw him. And

he went over to him and *stared* at him. And he saw the button on his shirt. A *red* button, *sewed* with a *needle* and with *black thread*, I heard my mother telling me that.

He was wearing a cap with — d'ye know the kind the *gardaí* [policeman] wear? — with a black *peak*... tweed trousers and a tweed vest with brown buttons. And a grey shirt and a red button on the shirt.

It's a long, long time since he left. But they say that he used to make a terrible whistle, down there on the shore. Three times. You would hear it anywhere, that man's whistle. They say that man was drowned or something. He was there all the time.

But one St Patrick's day, a man went over there and he threw a glass of whiskey down there where he used to be standing, down there at the edge of the boats.

And they say that from that day to this day he never was there.

* * *

The year before, Mary McClafferty had told me a good bit about her life as a girl and as a married woman. There were now only a few days left before I had to leave Tory and it was time to ask Gráinne if she would tell me her story as well. The way she began — 'I had sheeps to watch' — reminded me of Patsy Dan's comparison of the sheep on the island now and in the old days: '... a completely different type of sheep now than they used to be on the island in my early days. They're called mountain sheep and their breed have come from the mainland, and they are very, very hungry sheep indeed. In my early days, the type of sheep they used to have on the island, they were very *modest* sheep, so to say. You could call them island sheep. They weren't hungry at all, they could be fed on a small bit of land for ages... In those days the people weren't able to afford fencing and they were sure in watching them and not letting them down through the village or into any man's property...'

I had sheeps to watch.
By the sheepfold, round by the old graveyard, away

up the cliffs and, oh, everywhere with the sheeps. Sitting there watching them. I had a lonely time.

They would let them go everywhere in the winter, all through the island. But when the potatoes were set and corn was set and everything, you had to watch them. You couldn't let them inside the ditches at all.

Well, I left the sheeps then and I went to work over at William Doohan's. I went there in 1930 about when I was fourteen, and I used to be going every six months, up to 1934. I *wasn't* at school; at thirteen I left school. *You have to*, at that time.

And my first pair of shoes, I was sixteen years. There was a shop over here called Ben Duthie's shop. He got boots and shoes. My mother got me a pair there for ten shillings at that time, fifty pence they say now.

Ten shillings they were, that's my first pair of shoes.

Gráinne worked for the Doohans, 'old William, young William and the missus herself', from April until the end of October. She took care of the cows and calves and cleaned the byres. Indoors she washed up the dishes, helped old Mrs Doohan wash the clothes and, twice a week, churned the milk. 'They had their own potatoes, their own milk, their own butter and everything. They weren't buying much in the shop, only tea and sugar and flour they were well off in *that* kind of way. But we were poor, d'ye see, we hadn't got that... God rest them, they're all gone now.'

I knew that Gráinne had worked on the mainland. When there was a pause in the conversation, I asked her if she had found her job at a 'rabble'. Rabbles, or hiring fairs, probably began in Ulster and Donegal about two hundred years ago and ended some time after World War II. The system seemed to me to be similar to a slave market, for the young boys and girls who needed work were looked over by their prospective employers in much the same way as the cattle were being sold on the opposite side of the street. Once the requirements for domestic or farm help had been satisfied, the newly employed had to go with whoever hired them, whether they wanted to or not. They were given five shillings (the parents took the money home if they had come with their children), and were then brought to the pub for a drink. After which, their case or bundle was taken from them and not returned until the day they left their job. Gráinne told me that her mother was hired at the rabble in Letterkenny.

> Got hired with anybody that came and asked you. For six pounds. That's all she had. My mother worked hard on it, too.
>
> All the farms there — up in Strabane, up in Castlefin, and Newbuilding — used to be looking for Donegal girls, good working girls.
>
> There used to go a crowd from Tory there, a whole lot together of them. And they would *walk* in to *Letterkenny*, at that time.

Gráinne had her own experience of hard work:

> I left here on the eighth of April, 1935. A cousin of mine got this place for me, a farmer house down in Derry. Near Newbuilding. My mother left me down. And I didn't know nothing about *heavy* work at that time. Till I went there.
>
> I had to get up at six o'clock in the morning and have to milk seven cows. You would get no breakfast till you had everything done.
>
> And the first two days my hands all got swollen up. When I was three days there, I wasn't able to milk only two of them because my fingers got all swollen. I wasn't used to milking too much. But, I got into it, I got used to it.
>
> And I had to feed *nine big* pigs. Two buckets of gruel, potatoes and meal and feed.
>
> And ten wee small ones. I used to give them milk and a little light food. And then I would have to take two big buckets of boiled potatoes, and Indian meal — 'corenda' we called it at that time — and mix it up with spuds and feed the wee heifers with it.

And I had to go out then and carry nine or ten big wraps of corn on my back, up to a big field where there was more animals that wasn't in at all.

And one day I went up. And I had six or seven of them on my back with me, on a rope. And I heard this big thing, mooing and coming. A bull that broke out!

And *I* run, as fast as I can, and up the ditch, and I left my stockings behind me, on the ditch. And I got all scraped. I was covered with blood. And I was lucky. The bull could kill me.

You had to finish all the work before you'd get your breakfast. You'd get a wee bowl of porridge. And a slice of bread. And a mug of tea. And that's all. Till dinner time.

You'd get your dinner at one then. Potatoes and meat and soup. You'd get tea in the evening and then you get a plate of porridge around eight o'clock at night. *I* didn't like the porridge at that time, but you have to eat it. The hunger would eat everything.

And one night I was in bed. I had a wee room of my own in the back, and I heard this scraping coming. I rose up, and I lit a match and I lit the candle. There was no light in that house.

What was it but a big rat! And I was afraid of my life of it.

And this is what I am going to tell you, about the holy clay.

And it went up on the window and came down again. And I was afraid of it, but I had nothing to kill it. I had no stick, no nothing.

So I opened my case, the middle of the night, and I got the holy clay. And I sprinkled the holy clay down, where it came out of.

And I went up to bed then, I didn't hear the noise no more. So I slept on then till I was wakened up at six; *he* used to knock the door at six.

And when *I* got up at six and opened the back door, this big rat was dead outside the door.

He said to me, the master said, 'Oh,' he said, 'we have a very good dog,' he said. 'The dog killed it.'

I said nothing.

From that day till I left, I never heard the rat.

Apart from outside work there was much to be done in the house as well. Endless buckets of spuds to be washed and then boiled in a big tub in the kitchen. A huge churn had to be cleaned. 'There was a wee ladder going up to it. I had to go up them four steps with buckets of hot water and throw them in this thing, and *go into* it myself and wash it and scrub it. And then throw cold water on it and drain it.'

Gráinne helped to make butter, pounds of it, and wash many dozens of eggs before putting them in boxes. All these and a large cask of buttermilk had to be ready on Friday evening to be sent to Derry. 'It was terrible hard work,' said Gráinne. 'Oh, I was killed in it. And I got four pounds in pay.' Gráinne was in Derry in 1935; in 1936 she went over to Mountcharles to work in a hotel. The work was hard, but it was 'clean'.

She came home in 1938 and was married to Patrick in 1939. He had already built the house they live in now, and they moved into it immediately. Gráinne was fortunate. As she said, 'Way back it was big families. Every house here there was nine or ten. The women used to go in with the old people, and the children were reared with their grannies and that. But later on, in my young days, the last ones they wouldn't like to go to live with them. They stayed in their own houses, surely. The most of them.'

In describing the time when their mother was first married, Gráinne told me about the island midwives. They performed their task well, but, she said, 'Many's a one that died with babies here. I don't remember it, but I heard my mother talking about it.'

There were problems other than childbirth, however. Alfred McFarland wrote, 'By the census of 1841, it appears that the island then contained 85 families making in all 399 [people]... in 1851 the population amounted to about 400. Of late years the number of inhabitants has been kept in check by a singular malady, that visits nearly all the children. It is called the "Head-fall". In 1849 the proportions of death from this disease alone to that of births was about eight to nine.'

The same disease, though its milder form, was sometimes found on the coasts; no one at that time seemed to know its cause, or cure. By 1852, however, the number of incidences began to decrease. On McFarland's visit to the island in 1849 he noted that, apart from the sickness, 'Tory is in general very healthful, and enjoys what the geographers call "a salubrious clime".' I told Gráinne that I had read about the illness of babies called 'head-fall'.

> We call it the headaches.
>
> I heard my mother talking about it. Nearly all the babies died with it. It was happening for a long, long time.
>
> They would *die* when they were a year, and they would die when they were two years. They would die *young*. Pain in their heads.
>
> Aye. There were no doctors coming in, that time.

'McFarland also wrote about Paddy Heggarty,' I remarked. 'He said he lived in the cottage, over in the east end.' McFarland had written, 'Until lately, the cottage and the Lighthouse were the only buildings in Tory that did not form an immediate part of one of the three towns.'

> Wee Paddy Heggarty. I heard about him too. Aye.
>
> He lived in the big house was built over there. I suppose the walls are still there. 'Twas a big house. *Hotel.* They were making bed and breakfast in it — oh, way back. Well, I heard my father saying — his father knew him — he was a schoolteacher here and he was living over on the far east of the island.
>
> And at that time the people of Tory were making poteen. And Paddy was well up with the guards [police], and he used to put a light up in the upper window.
>
> And when the guards would see the upper light, they

knew that poteen was on the island. And they would come in, in the middle of the night, and rob the wee houses where they were making the poteen.

They would catch the ones making it, and throw away everything they had, and take them away. Arrest them. This was carrying on a long, long time before the people knew what was wrong.

There was a currach out fishing, this evening, and they saw Paddy putting the light up in the window. And the guards arrived that night so they knew that was the plan he had on them, reporting the poteen. I suppose he was getting money from the guards for doing that.

My grandfather was arrested. They took the whole poteen off him, and they charged him money for it.

I saw his [Heggarty's] daughter Máire Bheag. I was in with my mother with her, aye, on the mainland.

She had a kind of big dresser with delf on it. And she had a wee chair at the foot, and she used to go up on the chair to take down the things.

She had an old-fashioned head, and small hands like a wee girl, like a girl about twelve or thirteen, and the feet the same. And she wore old-fashioned clothes, did ye know, dark black clothes, but a wee kind shawl on her back.

And mixed grey hair, all bundled in the back. A very old-fashioned face. The day I was there I took in turf and I put on a fire for her. He died a few years after that, *créatúr*.

* * *

'You were saying,' I reminded Gráinne, 'that in your mother's time the women were still wearing the long skirts, down as far as their shoes. It must have been difficult to do so much hard work in those heavy skirts.'

Oh, they used to do it. Putting out seaweed and everything, down the shore.

My granny was telling me. She was over putting out

seaweed, over there where the pier is now; and she was expecting a baby and she came home and went to bed and the baby was born.

She was *working* to the very minute. She was telling me that. Oh, they were hard days.

And they wouldn't stay in bed only four or five days. Well, they wouldn't go outside but they would be in the house. They would do the work in the house.

And they wouldn't give you nothing else but oatmeal bread and oatmeal porridge. On *this* island they wouldn't. But if you go out to the hospital.

I had a baby born in Letterkenny hospital. And I got meat and soup. On Sunday. And I was afraid to take it because of the habit at home.

And the nurse made me eat it, so; potatoes and everything.

But they wouldn't give them that here, on this island anyhow. That's the habit they have.

* * *

'*Every* house, there was weaving [spinning]. My granny and my auntie used to be doing that *all* the time,' said Gráinne. 'Making thread, making jerseys and stockings for the men, with sheep's wool. Every house was at that. The women were working hard that time. They had to card that wool on two cards, and make rolls of it to that it would be easy leading into the wheel.'

Nabla Doohan of Whitefield in East Town, whose mother died when she was a child, was so small when she started using her mother's spinning wheel that she had to stand at the wheel to work. She told me that with the yarn she spun, she knit socks and jerseys for her father and brothers, using a diamond, or cross-and-diamond [Tory], pattern for the jerseys. These were different from jerseys on other islands in that they had a collar that opened on the left side, with three white buttons.

Patsy Dan said that every island had their own jersey pattern. Gola, Arranmore, Inishmaan, Inishfree and Tory (all off the Donegal coast) fished together, 'moving with the herrings' in

Magheraroarty Bay and off Tory. The fishermen could always tell from which island a man came by the pattern of his jersey.

I told Gráinne that Seán Ó hEochaidh had said that the fishermen of those days wore only the heavy stockings, no boots. She agreed, in part.

> Socks and, well they used to wear wellies [wellingtons]. And leggings on their shoes, kind of leathery leggings, buckles on the side of them.
>
> Keep their trousers clean... [the women] wore shawls, to Mass. *Every one* of them, black shawl at Mass.
>
> In my young days I saw it. There wasn't a coat in the chapel, only all black shawls. And the hair all folded in the back.
>
> It was nice, all combed back and a big bun in the back. That's all the women's style on Tory at that time. And [at chapel] the women always on the right side and the men on the other side. *Where they still are.* That never changed on Tory. Never changed.

* * *

I did not always take a tape recorder with me when I visited Gráinne. There were times when we just sat and chatted about events of the day and not of times past. But sometimes she would be reminded of something she thought would interest me and the next afternoon I would come back with recorder in hand.

> Was I telling you about my father when he was a lad and his granny died?
>
> He got up one night to go to the toilet — at that time they had buckets in, in the old houses — and he went down. And the hands came on him. The two cold hands on his eyes.
>
> And he couldn't move, and he was trying to struggle, and he couldn't squeal, and he couldn't call out because his mother and father were sleeping in the kitchen. At the end of the house.

And they let go then and he shouted. And his father got up and said, 'What's wrong?'

And he said, 'An old woman was holding me.' He'd seen the skirt.

And his father said, 'Oh, that was her.' His mother.

That was funny. And *her* dead. And she was holding him, her hands on her eyes. That was going in those times, not now. You don't hear anybody talking about that now.

Now my wee girl, she was two years old when she died.

And she took a sore throat, and I was sitting up that night with her. And I left the cradle here outside the bed, and at two o'clock the cradle started rocking.

And I said to myself, 'That's funny. There's no cat in, there's no dog in, there's nothing in. And why is the cradle moving?'

And I wakened up Patrick and I told him, says I, 'Do you hear the cradle going?'

'No,' says he.

'Well,' says I, 'the cradle's going for ten minutes.'

And the next day she got very bad. And she died the next day.

* * *

I remembered Patsy Dan telling me, 'Nobody wants trouble, that's the way it has been in the Tory community; they never liked trouble in many ways and they don't want trouble among themselves either... ' They were, no doubt, just trying to get along together in a small community; but perhaps also they were afraid that an aggrieved person might 'curse on them'. Gráinne had her own taste of cursing when she was young.

Aye, they were down on their knees cursing.

We took the flu into Tory once. Me and Feidhlimí were out in the country [on the mainland] and Feidhlimí caught the flu. And in here, then the flu spread.

And there was a woman up here — oh, she's dead and gone now — and she went up to the grotto and went down on her knees, cursing on me and Feidhlimí. Cursing us.

And I was told about it. And I went up to the priest. I put a pound in my pocket and I told the priest to say a Mass for myself and Feidhlimí, that the woman was cursing on us.

'Well,' he says, 'take it easy, don't say nothing and don't you curse back,' he said. 'They'll get the revenge of their own curses. It'll all come back on top of them,' he said to me.

They would curse the animals, too, oh aye, they would. Oh, that was happening here too, long, long ago. But that has stopped. The people are not as bad now as then.

Cows, in particular, were never safe from the revenge of disgruntled fairies. Bridget Doohan told me that the most common form of sickness in cows, caused by fairies, was *caitheamh* (throw, shot). 'There were times,' said Bridget, 'when the fairies did not like the cow to eat *fresh, green grass*', and so shot her with an elf-shot, a special dart. The result was a fever which was first suspected when the cow lost her appetite, and became more certain if the cow began to grow visibly shorter. To be sure that this was the correct diagnosis, however, one measured the cow from the end of her tail to the tip of her nose, using the length of one's arm — from the elbow to the end of the longest finger — as a measuring stick. If the measurement did not come out evenly, it was a sure sign that the cow was indeed feverish. The usual cure, as related by Bridget and by Jimmy Duggan, was to take a burning sod from the fire with iron tongs and pass it three times around the cow's belly. Then the still glowing turf was put below the cow's head and smashed out while, at the same time, a Hail Mary was said or the sign of the cross made. Gráinne's mother, as usual, took no short-cuts.

My mother came in this day. She said, 'The cow is very sick. I must try and make that cure *for* her.'

She measured the cow first. She caught the cow's tail — I saw her doing it — and put her elbow on it, and up to the head of the cow. Once and then the second time. And the third time she had an extra one.

She went out, then, and she took the tongs and a lump out of the fire *out* with her. So she started on the cow down at the tail up to the head, three times. And around her belly, *three* times. With the tongs and the red sod, around.

And then she went up under her head, and *smashed* it with her shoe and held the cow's head on top of it.

And then she got a drink for the cow. And she threw a penny into it. And the dust from the pan, and the dust from the pot and kettle. And the cow drank it, and the cow got okay.

If she went into the byre in the morning, and the cow wouldn't like to eat the corn or nothing, my mother would catch her ear.

And if her ear was cold, she said the cow would have some infection. And she used to catch the end of her skirt, and she would say, 'In the name of the Father, the Son, and the Holy Ghost', *three* times. And slap the cow with her skirt.

That's a cure my mother had; oh, many's a time I saw her doing that.

And after you finish milking, you used to make the sign of the cross [with the thumb] on the cow's back. With the white thing that's on top of the milk, aye the foam.

The same as when they're *blessing* themselves. It's the thumb, oh, it's the thumb. Some people do *that* [using thumb and forefinger] but my mother she used to always use the thumb.

Not now, but in the old days. Whatever the reason we don't know.

* * *

Alfred McFarland recorded that 'when there is a dance [on Tory] they moisten it with the best of generous liquor; for a considerable bulk of their grain is bestowed on poteen, a potable spirit, for which there is a ready demand, both at Torry and on shore… In one fortnight, in the autumn of 1848 upwards of forty gallons of native growth were taken to a single public house on the coast.'

Dónal Doohan described the making of poteen in the old days when the barley was ground into meal between two stones (querns). 'That's in the *old* time; ah, they're quicker now.' Like Dan Rodgers, he thought green apples made the best whiskey. 'Boil them in a pot, them green apples, d'ye know. They're no good eating, bad taste to them, but they will make the best of whiskey.' And he was most particular about the amount of heat necessary for the yeast. 'You put a bit of yeast in the hot water, in a can, and put it on the fire and give it a wee heat. Not *much*. A wee heat, ohhhh, you burn it if you give it too much heat, and it wouldn't work. The same as a clucking hen will be laying on eggs; that's the heat you want on the yeast.'

Gráinne Bhrianaí was pleased to give me the recipe.

> I'll tell you now how I make it.
>
> I was out in the country and I bought a packet of oatmeal. And I bought four pounds of currants and took them in with me. And six or seven pounds of sugar. It was cheap at that time. That's a long time ago.
>
> I took it in here; and poor Willy was alive at that time. I said to him, 'I took in currants and sugar and oatmeal. We should steep it.'
>
> 'Well,' he said, 'wait,' he said, 'and I'll get another package of meal.'
>
> And so he got another package of meal and some sugar. And we steeped it in here in the bath, in the back. For sixteen days. And then we squeezed the dross.
>
> One night, we were all here, this place was full, but we were squeezing in the back. Nobody saw us! And I had a churn at that time, ye know the churn you churn milk in. I said to Willy, 'The churn will do it.'

And we put yeast on in then and put the yeast in a can beside the fire, in hot water — as warm as the milk from a cow, my mother used to say — till it starts getting bubbly.

So then when I saw it starting bubbling, I just threw it into the churn. And that was going for four or five days. And then it lie down. Nicely.

So, we got the still then and empty it into the *ciltí* [still]. We had *seven and a half* bottles of whiskey.

That's double. We took it down first single and then we put it back and we had it double. It's better when it's double. Strong. Each one of us has three and a half bottles.

Oh, it was *great* crack. It was great crack. But the worst of it, Willy got drunk. [Gráinne giggled at the thought.] But I hid the bottles.

I *cured* my donkey from it. Wait till I tell you.

The donkey got sick, and I had this, the poteen, upstairs. And somebody said to me, 'If you had a glass of whiskey, it would cure her.'

She was very sick. I thought to *myself*, 'I have better stuff than *that*.' But I said, 'I have whiskey.'

I put a drop of black tea through it [the poteen]. I gave it to the donkey. About three glasses of it.

It was the *slaghdán* [common cold] she had. Donkeys used to get cold, their head would block up with the yellow stuff. She got rid of it. It made her sneeze and she put out the whole lot. She was better.

And the stuff that lie down in the bottom [of the still], it's like real yellow mud. But if you put that in bottles it'll do another throw for you, if you're making poteen again. It's the same yeast.

And Pádraig here, put it into bottles. And one night we were sitting here and we heard the 'bomb' going. Somebody said, 'What's *that*?' One of the boys said, 'Somebody threw a stone in the house.'

No. It wasn't. It was the bottle went. It *burst*! It was that strong. It *burst* the bottle. Aye. [Gráinne's eyes twinkled and she chuckled.]

'There were certainly great carryings-on on Tory in those days,' I said.

'Oh, it was great. Oh, many's a time I was over with Johnny Dixon making poteen, too, God rest him. They're all dead now. He used to call me Kitty Daly. But the poteen they were making there, it wasn't that good, it wasn't that strong.'

'Dónal liked green apples for making poteen,' I remarked.

'Oh, aye. Green apples are good. But I still think they would rather make beer than poteen. You can't beat the blackcurrants. *Blackcurrants.* And *sugar.* And *oatmeal.* Aye.'

Gráinne's eyes had a far away look in them. 'You're getting thirsty just thinking of it,' I teased as I got up to go. The sound of Gráinne's delighted laughter followed me out the door.

Patsy Dan Rodgers
(b. 1945)

I did not arrange these stories in the order in which they were told to me, and the age of the storyteller does not have any bearing on the sequence. But for various reasons I placed Dónal Doohan, now in his ninetieth year, first, and so it seemed fitting that I end with Patsy Dan Rodgers who, in his early forties, is the youngest of those who talked to me about Tory.

Patsy and his wife, Kathleen, were the islanders I first met on Tory. They were then living in a rented house at the head of the West Town Pier, but later moved to a very old house on Upper Lane, not far from Patsy's parents. It had been loaned to them as a temporary dwelling, until the council house, long-promised by the Donegal County Council, would be built. After over two years of hope and disappointments the new house was finally completed. It stands on a piece of high ground beyond West Town, and is compact, snug and warm. When the winds are strong around Creiggan House, as it is called, they make a sound outside the walls like a host of lost souls crying to be let in but, unlike the old house, there are no cracks or crevices through which they can enter. It is a longer walk now from where I stay, but I continue my habit of spending the last part of every evening with Patsy and Kathleen. I do not mind the distance and the only thing I need fear after dark on Tory is bad weather.

The stories Patsy told me began more as clarifications of subjects already discussed with others than as his own oral history. 'Clarify' is one of his favourite words and to do so is an undertaking he regards as a necessity. Knowing this, I plagued him with questions, sometimes while sitting in his house on Tory, more often by letter or tape from the United States.

'How many wells are there on the island?' I would write.

'Where are they, and what are they called?' (There are ten wells, all still used for drinking-water, and I know all their names.) On tape, 'Tell me more, *please*, about the waterman... about children's games... about the Inishbofin ghost boat... about the elephant...'

He was generous with his responses and, in between answering my questions, he sent news of Tory. I was supplied with a fine fund of information. Patsy is one of four Tory painters. Two others, Ruairí Rodgers and Anton Meenan, also live on the island; Michael Finbar Rodgers lives on the mainland. They are the second generation of Tory primitive artists, and of these Patsy is probably the best-known at the present time. It was Derek Hill, the internationally known portraitist and landscapist, who was responsible for initiating the school of primitive painting, beginning with the work of the two elderly Dixon brothers. He is also responsible over the years for arranging art exhibitions in Ireland, Scotland and Paris, with more planned for the future. He himself has painted on Tory since the 1950s and, when on the island, stays in his small, simple hut (the last remnant of the old Lloyd's signal station) on the edge of the cliffs near the lighthouse.

The original artists, those who 'competed' with Derek Hill, were James Dixon, who painted prolifically; John Dixon, who finished only five pictures in his painting career; and James Rodgers, known as the 'Yank' because he had been to America where he had painted a picture of the Susquehanna River. Patsy Dan described Derek Hill's first meeting with James Dixon.

> Around 1956-57, I remember well, a gentleman called Derek Hill came out here to Tory Island. He stayed in the village the first couple of years, I believe... I could hardly say that he has missed a summer on the island since 1956. So I would dare say that he was on the island roughly two to three years when he was painting, one Sunday morning, down below our church — at the Big Strand, we call it. And immediately after Mass, one of the islanders walked down and was all excited looking at

Derek Hill painting this view of Tory, right across the harbour, so they say.

And then Derek Hill knew that one of the islanders was looking at what he was doing. So he turned around and said 'Good morning.' And the islander said 'Good morning' as well. And he [Derek Hill] says, 'What do you think of my painting?' And James Dixon the islander, who we are talking about, was smoking a pipe, pushing down the tobacco. So, 'Well,' he says, to answer back Derek Hill, 'I think I could do better myself.'

So that's how the primitive painting and the primitive school of art started on Tory. So anyway, Derek Hill walked all the way down from the hut again and went over to James Dixon. And he says, 'Look here, if I send you the materials, the brushes and the paints, will you start painting?'

'Well,' James Dixon says, 'I'm sure I will,' he says. 'But look here,' he says, 'send out nothing more than a few tubes of paint to me.'

'My God,' Derek Hill says, 'do you not want brushes and so on?'

'No,' he says. 'I will manage the brushes,' he says. 'Because I have a horse up in the field and he has a long tail,' he says, 'and I will make the brushes myself out of that tail,' he says.

So he was really meaning every word that he was saying. So James Dixon started day after day lashing away at his paint, getting down to his art work. And every day and every week was passing; and little he thought himself that each and every one of his paintings would speak a mile out for itself — and so did at the end.

* * *

Over quite a period of time I have watched Patsy and Kathleen's four children grow increasingly 'old-fashioned' (mature) and have seen them playing with various toys befitting their particular ages, as well as watching television. When I was a child, of course, there was no television; we seldom even listened to a radio. Apart from being read to by my mother every day, and going on frequent and wonderful expeditions with my father — either on foot through the surrounding countryside or driving in the Model-T Ford two-seater — my sister and I invented most of our own amusements. This was in a comfortable setting, not far from Philadelphia. I wondered what children on Tory used to do to entertain themselves.

Madge Rodgers played with other small girls on a see-saw made from a barrel with a plank across it. Bridget Doohan from the west and Nabla Doohan from the east told me that they played with dolls which they made themselves out of rags, or sometimes stones, with the faces painted on. Nabla liked to play with the dogs and cats and particularly with the lambs. The little girls jumped rope to the tune of 'Ring-around-the-rosy', played hide and seek, and both boys and girls joined in the game called 'Duck-a-rainey' or 'Duck-on-the-rainey', in which a stone was put on a rock and other stones thrown at it in an effort to knock it off. And in the evenings there was always the very frightening ghost and fairy stories told by their parents and their parents' friends as they sat around the fire.

Patsy told me of two games that he and his best friend particularly enjoyed. The first was making 'paint'. They would steal some ink from the schoolhouse, 'there was no scarcity of blue ink at all', and a handful of flour from the kitchen, 'which was scarce enough at the time.' They would put the handful of flour in a small paint can, add a full tin of water and the requisite number of drops of ink, mix it well, put the lid on and leave it for a day or two. They would have up to a dozen of these small tins which they would then sell to the other small boys as 'blue paint'; the price was a penny, two a penny and sometimes a threepenny bit.

Another favourite game of Patsy's was what he called Boat Rope. He and a friend would tie a length of rope around their waists and then walk in single file, the boy at the back dragging a sea-rod behind him, pretending that it was the tiller and that he was steering the boat. They would carry with them a can filled with empty barnacle shells and along with these a few dozen 'pennywinkles' (periwinkles). As they walked, or 'sailed', towards the lighthouse they would stop at intervals and set down a small pile of barnacles by the side of the road. Under a few of the piles they would put a periwinkle. The following day they would collect them. When they picked up a pile that had a periwinkle under it they would say, 'Oh, this is a lobster pot that we've got a lobster in it!' And when they came to a pile without a periwinkle they would exclaim, 'Oh, this is a lobster pot — no lobster at all in this!' 'So,' Patsy concluded, 'we were saying the pennywinkles were the lobsters and the shells were the pots. And that is the story of the Boat Rope.'

* * *

On one of my visits to the Tory lighthouse, the lighthouse keepers, knowing of my interest in the light and its history, loaned me a book called *The Irish Lighthouse Service* by Dr T G Wilson. At the time of its publication in 1968, Dr Wilson was vice-chairman of the Commissioners of Irish Lights. In the chapter on Tory, Dr Wilson wrote:

> Tory Island is one of the pleasant places where one feels that anything can happen... A few years ago when the Commissioners were making their way across the island, their nostrils were assailed by a pungent odour from seaward. On making inquiries, they were informed that this emanated from the carcass of "the elephant" which was being buried, or rather being entombed in a mausoleum.

Dr Wilson was of the opinion that the elephant had probably been part of a circus, had died on shipboard and had been thrown over the side.

At home, later, I thought of this strange story, and decided that it was definitely in need of some clarification by Patsy Dan. I sent my request, as usual, by tape. I knew that in 1960 repairs were being made to the slip next to the west end pier and that, to save the expense of making large quantities of concrete, stones were brought over by tractor from Lough an Deas to build into the structure. I continue in Patsy's own words.

The foreman on the job was called Welsh, and the whole operation was going very well. And *in* the middle of everything one of the islanders — what we call one of the watermen — came over one morning with strange news, with very exciting news. As I was telling you already, those number of men we had going along the shore day by day, we call them watermen and we had about six of *those*. And one of them came over on such a morning in the year of 1960. And he got a word out immediately, after reaching the West Village, that there was a *huge* sea animal, washed ashore.

At this stage, the current, and the breeze and so on, the art of wind, have brought the sea animal to the west side of the lighthouse, on the beach. But it didn't come right up on the beach, because it was so *big* and so *huge*, and the tide was a bit out, so it got on the rocks. And then when the tide came in, early in the evening, that was the hour of excitement. Because the community got the opportunity to get more and more excited, every minute that was passing, until they could get a closer look at the animal. Almost *everybody* that was on the island, men and women, went over to see what kind of animal it was. And then they started arguing between themselves. Many saying that it was a huge giraffe, others saying that it was an elephant. Others were saying that it was a sea-animal, and that they couldn't get a name *for* it. So anyway, it was brought up and indeed, I can tell you in a very, very *poor* condition.

So the foreman and the workers then decided that if there wasn't some operation carried out, as far as this animal was concerned, within the next twenty-four hours or within the next forty-eight hours, that it could be very *dangerous* to the community as a whole. Because someone with very less experience of the whole thing might be touching it with their hands and so and so forth. But anyway they decided the following day actually, to do something about it. And to put cement *on top of that animal*, just as the sea left it in its position, more or less at the bottom of the beach, so to say.

Then when the tide went out the following day they all went over: the tractor, up to thirty men *and* the foreman, and they started working immediately. So above the beach, actually, they were able to mix the concrete. And they were able to get the gravel also from the beach, *near* the animal itself. So they started mixing right away and they averaged that *three ton* of concrete went on top of it. And we thought actually that the coffin, the grave or whatever, the cover, would last for *many*, many years to come. But in a matter of six or seven years, I dare say, it was all in *bits*. Nothing of it was left.

I had to wait until I returned to Tory, a month after getting Patsy's tape, to find the answer to a question I had forgotten to ask. 'How,' I enquired with great interest, 'did you finally discover that it was an elephant?' 'To be quite honest with you,' said Patsy, 'I think, as a matter of fact, that they're still puzzled over that.'

Patsy had promised to tell me the old, well-known story of the ganger and *cloch aclaidhe*, the large boulder near the lighthouse wall that was used as one of the stations on the *turas* (literally 'journey', part of the ritual of the cursing stone). When I arrived at his house as planned, I found that he was off on some errand, but Kathleen was there and, as the children were playing outside and everything was quiet, I asked her to tell me more about the *turas*, something perhaps that she had heard from her father. Her father, Johnny Doohan, is as old as Dónal and has as many memories of times long past; he is, however, even more deaf than Dónal and is not fluent in English. Sometimes Kathleen asks him questions for me and then translates the answers. 'In the old days,' Kathleen began, 'the women, if they were going to make the *turas*, they had to get up very early in the morning and they had to go with the sun.' This I knew, but she continued with a fact that I had not heard before. 'They would be wearing red blouses and black skirts, and anyone with long hair would have it down their back… '

In the nineteenth century, Mgr James Stevens described the Tory women as 'noble, tall and dark-featured'. As Kathleen spoke, I saw them with great clarity as they walked barefoot around the island; red blouses bright against the grim rocks, rosaries clasped tightly in their hands, their long hair flying in the wind. But before I could hear more, Patsy returned, much to his wife's relief as she dislikes talking into a tape recorder. After sitting down for a few minutes to catch his breath, Patsy told me the story of the man called Little.

> Now the name of this foreman, or ganger they call them nowadays, that was looking after the workers when those walls surrounding the lighthouse was *built* was Little. A man called Little, down from the heart of Ireland, so to say.
> And he was warned by a number of the islanders, when working, not to touch this stone. And he said, 'Oh well,' he said, 'this stone is very temptational. And it's big and I'm going to blast this stone.' So some of the workers got very angry with him, indeed, but he says, 'Well,' he says, 'you have to get the anger on one side. This,' he says, 'is my job and I have to do this.'
> So then anyway he went ahead with blasting until the stone went up to bits. And they warned him already, and also said in their statement to him that it *would* not be in any way — they used another word — than unlucky. They told him that something might happen to himself or a number of the workers. So anyway, there was a fellow there with a cart and horse. And *he* was ordered by the foreman, by Little, to go down and carry the bits up on the horse's cart. And with that he went down, because he was in need of the money like the rest, and couldn't go off the job, so to say. When the cart was loaded, the horse went *mad*. Went *furious*! And even the workers couldn't keep him back. He went *mad* in the cart, but they got over that one way or another and controlled him one way or another. A couple of days after that Little took sick. Very ill indeed, and he had to

be brought to the mainland. And within *eight* or nine days the word came that Little had died.

* * *

During my frequent visits to the Rodgers' house, Patsy told me a variety of stories. Some he had heard from the older people, others he had experienced himself. I am sorry that I cannot include them all. Many of his clarifications, however, are already scattered through the pages of the book. The last story in this chapter is one of my favourites because it involves Patsy and, offstage, his father, Dan. When I mentioned one day that I was going to ask Dan for his recipe for poteen, Patsy was interested. 'It must have been up to fifteen years, at least,' he said, 'since I saw it last brewed. What we would call the *right* poteen, brewed by the old people. Nowadays they don't brew poteen as good as they used to twenty, thirty years ago, when I was a young chap. And it's not the same ingredients at all that they use now. My father was very fond of cooking apples, as green as you could get them and going quite rotten. And also treacle, and also raisins if he could get his hands on them. And then — if you hadn't got barley — potatoes going rotten as well.'

When the apples, and potatoes or barley, had been prepared, soaked in warm water and then pressed to get out all the liquid; when the other ingredients, including the yeast, had been carefully added, the whole 'slush', looking like Scotch broth as Patsy described it, would be put into a barrel, filled right up to the top. As it began to ferment, 'it was all in *bubbles*, you could see the bubbles coming up: like throwing someone out the west end pier, and then the bubbles would start coming up once he would get to the bottom. And the barrel was singing, along with that.' With this graphic introduction, Patsy began the story of a never-to-be forgotten Sunday evening when he was sixteen.

> I remember one evening in particular — it was a Sunday evening, a *beautiful* Sunday evening it was, too. And at that time, as it is still today, there would be a Rosary going on in the chapel around six o'clock.
>
> And anyway, I knew my father had this barrel out in

one of the sheds and the barrel was hiding. There was more clamp-down for those who were brewing poteen at *that* time, in those years, than there is *now*. And funny enough to say.

But anyway, he told me of this barrel being at the back of the door in the shed. And he wanted me, because himself not having good eyesight at all, to keep on the look*out* and go over along with him now and then, so that I could see the stuff in the barrel, bubbling, so to say.

So, by this time all the ingredients were in the barrel and the yeast too. And they would give it at least three weeks to be in the barrel. As a matter of fact, once the twelve days would pass, twelve to thirteen days would pass, it would start bubbling. Day by day, more bubbles coming up in the barrel and so on.

But anyway, I went over this day which was Sunday and gosh, I can tell you, the barrel was in vibration, with the bubbles. And I said to myself, '*Nice enough*'. Although not knowing much about brewing poteen at all.

But anyway, the following day was Sunday and everything was going grand, and my father went for a walk, and my mother too. And then I decided to go to the church for Rosary, and a beautiful Sunday evening it was. At that time big crowds used to go to Sunday Rosary, in the evening.

And, as teenagers, a group of us used to run immediately *from* the chapel, once Rosary was over, and we would be the first over in the field to play football, or else back home before the middle-aged or old people. *Lucky* enough I came home that evening straight from the chapel; and as I was coming up at old Dan Doohan's house, gosh, before as a matter of fact, before I came to that house, this beautiful smell, *strong* smell of poteen, came to my nose.

And, it gave the feelings that my head got dizzy, so to say. But anyway, 'Gee,' I said myself — it was a complete stun at that minute — and I said to myself, 'My goodness what is this? What is this type of smell coming across?' And as I walked then another few steps, coming round the corner less than ten yards to my home, I just met the whole stuff that was put in the barrel roughly three weeks before that, all coming down like *pure porridge*. Like *Scotch broth* coming *down* the road to meet me. And it was *all moving*, so to say. In other words, like this volcano that blows up, and then it comes all down in clabber. And, gee, I can tell you, and even though I was a teenager and well on the side of fun and so on, I got very, very excited. I *knew* damn well at the minute, that my father would be in trouble. So I knew that much anyway. And *gosh*, I ran home like hell, the other few yards home.

And I said, '*Anybody in?*' D'ye know.

And said to my mother, '*I'm here.*'

'And where is Daddy?' I says.

She says, 'I don't know where he is but he went out there a good while ago.'

'Oh,' I said to myself, 'he will be back in a *minute*, surely to goodness, when something is going wrong.' And she says, 'What is it?'

'Ohhhh,' says I. 'There's an awful smell of poteen going down to Dónal Beag's house.'

'Oh my God,' she says, '*I'm fainting.*'

'Oh well,' I says to her, '*you* won't be much good to me anyway. Come on out till you see,' and, gosh, she had to lean on the porch; there's a bevel around the porch at the bottom of the window, and she leaned on *that*. And she started to look at me and she was *sweating*.

And she said, 'Ohh, do something fast, do something fast, your father will be back and there will be *murder* on the island.' Ye know.

So anyway, William Rodgers had, lucky enough, two tractor loads of gravel from the beach which he got two or three days before that. He was to build something, some type of a wall or a small shed or something. I remember that anyway. And I just *dashed* into that load of gravel. And there was two loads there but it was all in one load, and I jumped on there, and *took* a bucket and *took* a shovel and I was, oh, *never before* that I worked, *nor since*, that I worked so hard, I can tell you.

And I must have put, *easy*, twenty to thirty buckets of gravel on it. *Right down the whole way*. And I was going down, filling up the bucket, coming up again, half full as a matter of fact, and just dumping it on, running down again and up and I was like that, *twenty*, *thirty* times at least. Up and down like a *yo-yo*.

But anyway, I can tell you I got really the better of it. So, the gravel had sucked it all in, so to say. So one could say, 'My goodness, you're building a nice path.' Or, 'You're preparing a nice path for someone special.' And then I took a broom-brush and I started. And that was the worst of it again, I was really sweating by this time.

And I had all the work almost done, up to the doorstep of my own house or to the door of the shed, when the *rest* came over from the churchyard. They would stay at the church, the older people, or the middle-aged class and would start chatting with one another and so on. And this had given me a great opportunity to be ready. And I remember anyway, the friends next door, as they came up close to my house, after coming over from the church, they were smelling away, sniff, sniff. 'My goodness, what is this *at all?* What has happened? Sniff, sniff. Somebody must have...' and all this was going on, ye know. And this is what they were at. And they didn't know *what* was on. Of course, they could see the dampness, but they would *never* have the second thought that it was a barrel of poteen and all the ingredients — that had blown its cap off, so to say.

It didn't just go out through the roof and nothing more. The barrel itself went to bits. And maybe only that it was a cement roof that was on the shed, it might have gone through. Because there was a good force in that, you know, when there was so much of yeast in it. Oh, there was a good lot of yeast.

A very dangerous tactic, too, that my father used to have. He would have so much *leavings* left after all this, and there was yeast in the leavings, too. The worst of the yeast, so to say, the whole strength of it. And he used to get this in bottles, *saving* it. Big brown bottles, big green bottles, all colour of bottles and, *gosh*, some day you would hear also a 'bang' in the shed, or in the henhouse or somewhere like that, you know. And the bottles just going to bits. That was an awful habit he used to have.

I felt quite breathless by the end of the story. 'I thought the real danger in making poteen was the unexpected arrival of the guards, not an explosion that would blow the roof off a shed,' I said.

'Which is quite true,' said Patsy.

Epilogue

The stories told to me have been written. I have lived with them for over six years, and with each re-reading I could hear again the voices of the storytellers and feel the special ambience of the rooms in which the stories were told. They, and the music I also taped, have provided me with a link to Tory when far away from the island. I feel not only a sense of accomplishment but also a sense of loss now that the book has been finished, but I trust my visits to Tory are not at an end — at least as long as I retain my ability to climb into a half-decker or keep my balance on the deck of the trawler. And the island itself, I hope, will continue to survive and will not succumb to the countless problems and difficulties that have resulted, sadly, in the evacuation of other Irish islands.

Bibliography

Bayne, Samuel Gamble. *On an Irish Jaunting-car through Donegal and Connemara.* New York and London, Harper, 1902.

Campbell Joseph. *Mearing Stones: Leaves from my Note-book on Tramp in Donegal.* Dublin, Maunsel, 1911.

Evans, E Estyn. *Irish Heritage. The Landscape, the People and their Work.* Dundalk, Tempest, 1942.

Fox, Robin. *The Tory Islanders: A People of the Celtic Fringe.* Cambridge, Cambridge University Press, 1978.

Hamilton, J N. *A Phonetic Study of the Irish Tory Island.* Belfast, 1974.

Harkin, William. *Scenery & Antiquities of North-West Donegal.* Derry, 1893.

Jobes, Gertrude, *Dictionary of Mythology, Folklore and Symbols.* New York, Scarecrow Inc, 1962.

Maguire, Very Rev Edward. *History of the Diocese of Raphoe.* Dublin, Browne and Nolan, 1920.

Mason, T H. *The Islands of Ireland.* London, 1936.

McDevitt, Rev James. *The Donegal Highlands.* Dublin, Murray, 1866.

McFarland, Alfred. *Hours in Vacation.* Dublin, E J Milliken, 1853.

O'Donovan, John. *Letters Containing Information Relative to the Antiquities of the County of Donegal Collected During the Progress of Ordnance Survey in 1834.* Dublin, 1926.

Ó hEochaidh, Seán. *Fairy Legends from Donegal.* Dublin, 1977.

Otway, Caesar. *Sketches in Ireland Descriptive of Interesting and Hitherto Unnoticed Districts in the North and South.* Dublin, William Curry, 1827.

Spenser, Edmund. *View of the State of Ireland.* Dublin, L Flin, 1763.

Stevens, Mgr James. *Illustrated Handbook of South-Western Donegal.* Dublin, 1872.

Westropp, T J. *Antiquarian Handbook Series,* no. vi. Dublin, 1905.

Wilde, Sir William Robert Wills. *Irish Popular Superstitions.* Dublin, J McGlashan, 1852.

Wilson, Dr T G. *The Irish Lighthouse Service.* Dublin, Figgis, 1968.

Index

A

adoption, 79
áiteanna uaisle, 43–6
alcohol, 93, 102–3, 120–1, 126, 162–4, 173–7
Arranmore, 65–6, 88, 157–8
artists, primitive, 166–7

B

Balor, xxiii, xxiv–xxv, xxvi–xxvii, 28–9
banshee, 6, 121
baptismal font, 135–6
Bayne, Samuel, xxx
'Bhó Chrúbach, An' (song), 129
books, 85, 114, 135
Brigid, St, 108, 145
Bunbeg, 88

C

California (liner), 104–6
Campbell, Joseph, xxiii–xxiv
Camusmore, 7, 129
Carroll, Bríd, 62
Casement, Sir Roger, xxx, 126
cats, 39, 49–51, 98, 127–8
census, 154
Child of Prague, 148–9
childbirth, 68–73, 139, 154, 157
Childers, President Erskine, 128
children's games, 168–9
cliff fall, 54–6
cloch aclaidhe, 171–3
clothing, 156–8
coffins, 108
Coll, James, 30
Colmcille, St, xxii–xxiii, xxiv, xxvii–xxviii, 91
  comes to Tory, 27–9, 133
  cursing stone, 32–3
  Temple of the Seven, 34
Conan, xxvi–xxvii, 91

Congested Districts Board, 60, 79, 100–2, 131
cows, illness in, 160–2
cú nimhe (poison hound), 27, 29–30
cures, 136–9, 160–2
currachs, 86–7, 129
'bird,' 92
Curran, Hugh, 87, 124–5
Curransport, 88, 97
cursing, 31–4, 159–60
  cloch aclaidhe, 171–3
  stone, 93, 129

D

de Valera, Eamon, 115, 128
dead-watch, 146–7
death
  of babies, 155
  crying, 121–4
  drowning, 16–17, 106–7, 144–5
  hammering, 46–7
  omens of, 42–3, 119, 143–5
depopulation, 67–8, 154
Derry, 127, 152–4
Diver, Denis, 129
Diver, Hughie, 51
Diver, Jimmy, 129, 139
Diver, John, 111–12
Diver, Margaret, 12
Diver, Willy, 42, 145–6
Dixon, James, 118, 166
Dixon, John, 74, 118, 164, 166
doctors, 87–8
Doherty, Patrick, 141, xii
Doohan, Bernadette, xii
Doohan, Bridget, 2, 68, 160, 168
Doohan, Dan, 174
Doohan, Donal, 1–9, xviii–xix, xxxi, 76, 85, 98, 106, 129, 133, 141, 171
  cats, 49–51
  cursing, 32–4

fairies, 40–1, 44–9
  lights, 42–3
  poteen, 162, 164
  reminiscences, 10–20
  sinking of *Wasp*, 21–7
  St Colmcille, 28–9
  whales, 38
Doohan, Edward, 6–7, 14
Doohan, Gráinne, 85
Doohan, Gráinne Bhrianaí, 120, 121–2
  childhood, 148–9, 150–1
  cures, 136–9
  cursing, 159–60
  fairies, 139–43
  poteen recipe, 162–4
  reminiscences, 134–64
  working life, 152–4
Doohan, Gráinne (Óg), 146, 159
Doohan, Jimmy, 67
Doohan, Johnny, 1–2, 9, 67, 171
Doohan, Kitty, 67
Doohan, Nabla, 157, 168
Doohan, Pádraig, 163
Doohan, Patrick, xii, 134, 154, 159
Doohan, Peggy, 42–3
Doohan, Roger, 15–16, 17, 106
Doohan, Seán Dónal, 2, 3
Doohan, William, 151
Dooley, Jimmy, 42
Dooley, Willy, 42, 75
Downey, Mrs, 62–7
Downings, 88, 89
Downs, Mrs, 62, 63
drowning, 16–17, 106–7, 144–5
Dublin, 7, 8, 61–7
Duggan, Anton, 143–4
Duggan, Billy, 21–3, 25
Duggan, Bríd Antoin, 67
Duggan, Denis, 12
Duggan, Father, 142
Duggan, Gráinne, 77–8
Duggan, Jimmy, 35, 135, 160
Duggan, Kathleen, 12
Duggan, Mary, 12
Duggan, Patrick, 12
Dunfanaghy, 85, 129
Duthie, Ben, 151

E

Egyptian cross, xxiv
elephant, 169–71
Ernan, St, xxviii
Evans, E Estyn, xxix
eye cures, 135–6

F

fairies, 38, 40–1, 43–9, 118–19, 139–43
  áiteanna uaisle, 43–6
  cow sickness, 160–2
  hammering, 141
  and poteen, 119–21
fairy shots, 118–19, 141, 160
Falcarragh, 38, 104, 129
family size, 101–2, 154
fishing, 10–11, 12–13
  fog, 99–100
  herrings, 88–9
  limpets, 86–7
  whales, 35–8
flotsam and jetsam, 89–90
fostering, 79
Fox, Robin, xvii, xxv, xxvii, xxviii–xxix, xxxi, 101, 114
  sinking of *Wasp*, 21
funerals, 30, 109–13, 115, 147–8

G

games, 168–9
Getty, Edmund, xxviii
ghosts, 5–6, 116–18, 149–50, 158–9
  crying, 121–4
glas gaibhlinn, xxiii–xxiv
Glassie, Professor Henry, xvi
Gola, 157–8
Gortahork, 88, 124
Greenport, 100, 148

H

Harkin, William, xxx, 9, 14, 18, 87
head-fall, 155
healing, 136–9
Heggarty, Máire Bheag, 156
Heggarty, Máire Phaidí, 124–5
Heggarty, Nelly, 124

Heggarty, Paddy, xxix, 124, 125–6, 155–6
Heggarty, Paidí, 106–7
Herison, Patrick, xxix
herring shoals, 88–9
Hill, Derek, 122, 148, 166–7, xii
hiring fairs, 151–2
holy clay, 34–5, 94–6, 153–4
housing, 60–1, 79–80, 101–2, 128, 131–2, 154
Hughie, Jennie, 71

I

Inishbofin, 53, 84, 85, 97, 146
Inishfree, 157–8
Inishmaan, 157–8
Inishmurray, 31
Inishowen, 100
Inishtrahull, 128
Inver Bay, 36–8
'It's not the morning' (song), 132–3

J

Joule, Benjamin St John Baptist, 100, xxii

K

keening, 19, 108–9, 112, 113, 121, 147–8
kelp, 60
Kincasslagh, 88, 89
knitting patterns, 157–8

L

Land Commission, 131
Leitrim, Earl of, 128
leprechauns, 46–7
Letterkenny, 152, 157
Liam Óg, 18–20
lighthouse, 169
lights
 as omen, 145–6
Liodán Mhuire, 99
Little, ganger, 172–3
Lloyd's house, 80, 122–3, 166
Lugh, xxiv–xxv, xxvi

M

McClafferty, Barney, 69, 74
McClafferty, Dan, 67
McClafferty, Gracie and Joe, 29
McClafferty, John Joe, 68
McClafferty, Mary, 7–8, 85, 109, 113, 121, 134, 149
 childbirth, 68–73
 in Dublin, 61–7
 parents-in-law, 74–6
 reminiscences, 52–78
 as servant, 56–60
 thatched house, 76–8
McClafferty, Mary (Óg), 68
McClafferty, Nabla, 69, 73–6
McClafferty, Pádraig, 53, 67, 69–71, 74, 75, 76
McClafferty, Paidí
 birth of, 69–73
McClafferty, Pat, 67
McDevitt, Rev J, xxiii
McDyer, Father, 69, 70, 72–3
McFarland, Alfred, xiv, xxi, xxiii, xxix, xxvi, xxx–xxxi, 124
 island work, 86
 population size, 154–5
 poteen, 162
 wishing stone, 130
McGinley, Dennis, 67
McGinley, Mary, 67
McGinley, Nellie, 67
McGinley, Pádraig, 67
McGinley, Tadhg, 62
McGinty's motor, 54
McGonigle, Father, 74–6
'McPherson's Wedding' (song), 2–4
McRory, Donnell, 91
McVeagh, Nurse, 68–9, 71, 72
Magheraroarty, 30, 85, 88, 96–7, 97, 124, 125, 158
Maguire, Dr Edward, xvii–xviii, xxii–xxiii, xxviii, 91
Mason, TH, 28, 31, 87, 89
Mayo, County, 18–20
Meenacladagh, 106–7
Meenan, Anton, 166, xiii
Meenan, Kate, 139

Meenan, Kitty, 67
Melmore (steamer), 14–15
Mooney, Dan, 67
Mooney, Mickey, 54–5
Mountcharles, 154

N

'Níl Sé 'na Lá' (song), 132–3

O

Ó Catháin, Séamus, 49
Ó Colm, Fr Eoghan, xvi–xvii
Ó Dubhagáin, Eamonn, 129
Ó hEochaidh, Seán, 36–8, 43–4, 94, 95, 118, 158
Ó Péicín, Fr Dermot, 20
O'Donnell, Kate, 7–8
O'Donnell, Manus, xvii–xviii, xxii–xxiii, 34
 Colmcille, 27–8
O'Donovan, John, xxv–xxvi, 28, 90–1
O'Dugan, 28–9
Oillil mac Boadan, 27–8
Otway, Caesar, xxvii, xxxi

P

Petrie, George, 91
Port an Churraigh, 106
Port Deilg, xxiv–xxv
Portadoon, 47–9, 149–50, xxv
poteen, 93, 102–3, 119–21, 143, 155–6, 162–4, 173–7
prayers, 138, 161
pregnancy, 68
priests, 61, 66, 73–4, 96–7, 112, 125, 131
 wakes, 110–11

R

rabbles, 151–2
Ranafarste, 129
Rathlin Island, 125
rats, 94–6, 153–4
Raughter, Tommy, 37–8
red-haired woman, 98
registrar, 85, 127

Rodgers, Annie, 108, 115
Rodgers, Bernard, 127
Rodgers, Bridget, 84–5
Rodgers, Dan, xxiii, 53, 54, 55, 67, 75, 91, 129, 133, 162, 173
 reminiscences, 79–103
Rodgers, Denis, 84–5
Rodgers, Éamonn, xi–xii, 53, 89
Rodgers, Eilish, xi–xii, 52, 53, 89, 114, 119
Rodgers, Gráinne Joe, 69
Rodgers, James, 12, 166–7
Rodgers, Jimmy, 8, 109
Rodgers, Jimmy Sarah, 120, 142
Rodgers, John, 53, 54, 60
Rodgers, John Liam Feidhlimi, 85
Rodgers, Johnny, 53
Rodgers, Kathleen, 1, 47, 102, 121–2, 135–6, 165, 167, 171–2
Rodgers, Madge, 168, xviii
 reminiscences, 104–7
 shingles, 137–8
Rodgers, Mary Hughie, 110–11
Rodgers, Maureen, 104, 132
Rodgers, Michael Finbar, xiii, 166
Rodgers, Nelly Cormac, 73
Rodgers, Pádraig Óg, xv, xxix, xxx, 27
 crying, 123–4
 derivation of 'Tory,' xxxi
 education, 127
 funeral, 115
 ghosts, 116–18
 Paddy Heggarty, 125–6
 reminiscences, 113–33
Rodgers, Patsy Dan, 1, xi–xiii, xix, 2, 4, 5, 14, 35, 109, 121–3, 134, 150
 adoption, 79
 cursing, 31–2, 159
 fairies, 47
 holy clay, 95–6
 jersey patterns, 157–8
 poteen, 173–7
 reminiscences, 165–77
 wakes, 110–13
 watermen, 89–90
Rodgers, Paul, 115
Rodgers, Peggy, 8, 104, 136, 137–8
Rodgers, Ruairí, xiii, 104, 166

Rodgers, Seán, xxv, 104
Rodgers, Una, 53, 54, 60, 75, 113
Rodgers, William, 30, 53, 60, 85, 133, 175–6
   cliff fall, 54–6
round towers, 91–2

S

St Andrew's cross, xxiv
school, 11–12, 53–4, 81, 125, 127, 151
Scotland, 7, 8, 79, 80, 94–5, 146–7
sea animals, 35–8, 95–6, 169–71
sheep, 13–14, 150–1
Shiels, Mrs, 56
shingles, 137–8
shipwrecks, 89–90, 104–6, 148. see also *Wasp*
slua sí, 141–3
Spenser, Edmund, 108–9
Stevens, Mgr James, 9, 92, 172
storms, 14–18, 106–7
Sweeney, Father, 61
swimming, 17

T

Teampall an Mhórsheisir, 34
Teelin, 36
thatched house, 76–8
tobacco, 119, 140
Tory Island
   derivation of name, xxx–xxxi
   short history of, xxv–xxxi
Tory Island Letters, 114

W

wakes, 18–20, 99–100, 108–9, 110–12, 121, 147–8
Ward, Ellie, 60, 76, 126
Ward, Niall, xxix, 126
Ward, Séamus, xxiv, xxix–xxx, 13, 125–6
warts, 135–6
Wasp, HMS, 9, 93, xxii
   ballad of, 25–6
   sinking of, 20–7
watermen, 89–90, 170
West Town, xxiv
Westropp, T J, xxiii
whales, 35–8, 96
Whoriskey, Biddy, 79, 80
Whoriskey, Eoghan, 74
Whoriskey, Hudaí, 102
Wilde, Sir William, 38, 142, 149
Wilson, Dr T G, 169
wind, calling up, 124
wishing stone, 129–31
women's work, 82–4, 156–8

Y

yawls, 88–9